To

From

Date

STORIES OF *Comfort* TO WARM THE HEART

True Stories of Hope and Inspiration

EDITED BY JILL JONES

Guideposts

Stories of Comfort to Warm the Heart

ISBN-10: 0-8249-4527-1
ISBN-13: 978-0-8249-4527-5

Published by Guideposts
16 East 34th Street
New York, New York 10016
Guideposts.org

Distributed by Ideals Publications, a Guideposts company
2630 Elm Hill Pike, Suite 100
Nashville, Tennessee 37214

Guideposts and *Ideals* are registered trademarks of Guideposts.

Acknowledgments
Every attempt has been made to credit the sources of copyrighted material used in this book. If any such acknowledgment has been inadvertently omitted or miscredited, receipt of such information would be appreciated.

Scripture references are from the following sources: The Holy Bible, King James Version (KJV). The Holy Bible, New International Version®, NIV®. Copyright © 1973, 1978, 1984, 2011 by Biblica, Inc.™ Used by permission of Zondervan. All rights reserved worldwide. The New American Standard Bible® (NASB), Copyright © 1960, 1962, 1963, 1968, 1971, 1972, 1973, 1975, 1977, 1995 by The Lockman Foundation. Used by permission. The Holy Bible, English Standard Version® (ESV), copyright © 2001 by Crossway Bibles, a publishing ministry of Good News Publishers. Used by permission.

Cover and interior design by Thinkpen Design, Inc. | www.thinkpendesign.com

Printed and bound in China
10 9 8 7 6 5 4 3 2 1

Contents

Introduction

Into every life shadows fall—disappointment, loss, adversity, sickness. When those shadows come, we long for comfort, for the feeling of being held close, the sense of having something solid to cling to. In this reassuring collection of true stories, you'll find comfort from the experiences of others whose faith has carried them through the dark times, bringing healing to their hearts.

Wrap yourself in the warmth and hope of tragedies overcome, heartaches healed, and lives changed. You'll discover in these stories that God opens His arms to comfort us no matter what we are going through. Experience with John McLaughlin, a teenager who lost his father, that "I feel the gentle hand of God reaching out to take mine and I can, with deep belief, turn to Him for comfort. It gives a wonderful sense of peace."

Whether you've suffered a loss, are working through the reality of disappointment, or are learning to live again, you'll find inspiration and comfort in these pages and cherish the peace that comes from knowing your future is in God's hands.

A True Purpose

BY LISA VAN RYN

I sat across the desk from the head of the university's physical-therapy program. "You received an education degree six years ago but never worked as a teacher," she said, peering at my résumé. "You waitressed at Olive Garden then quit last spring. Help me understand why you want to learn to be a physical therapist."

I could tell she thought I was just another young person with no direction. A year ago she might have been right. I was happily living at my parents' home in Michigan, taking life as it came (or not). But that was before the accident. I took a deep breath. "Let me tell you," I said, "how I got here."

Five months earlier my little sister Laura was in a horrible crash. A senior at Taylor University in Indiana, she was riding in a van with eight other students and staff, returning from working at a college banquet. A semi crossed the interstate median and crushed the van. Five passengers died. Rescue workers found Laura's body fifty feet away, her purse nearby. Her injuries were so severe and disfiguring that the proximity of her purse was the only way paramedics could put two and two together and identify her.

My parents and I rushed to the hospital in Indiana, three hours away, where Laura lay in a coma. We lived by her side, praying for a miracle. My two younger brothers, Mark and Kenny, joined us as often as they could take time off from work. That first night in the ICU she looked like a mummy, her head wrapped in bandages, her sparkling blue eyes hidden behind bruised and swollen eyelids. About all that was recognizable were the tufts of blond hair sticking up through the bandages. My sister—the outdoorsy, athletic girl, the one I'd taught to play guitar—seemed far away, beyond my reach, but not beyond God's.

In a couple of weeks they took off some of the bandages. A few days later she opened one eye and slowly emerged from the coma. It was incredible—a front-row seat to God's healing power! The transformation was so amazing that some days it seemed like she was a different person.

Her recovery filled me with awe. God must have something pretty important planned for her—big enough to preempt death. I wondered if I was part of this plan too. Before the accident, just thinking about hospitals made me squeamish. Now, I was focused on helping Laura. I quit my waitressing job to be with her, assisting with her physical therapy and just talking to her, even though she couldn't say anything back yet.

Three weeks after the accident we moved Laura to a rehabilitation center in Grand Rapids, Michigan, only forty minutes from our home. She was doing well enough that we felt comfortable sleeping at home. Each morning I leaped out of bed to get to the center for Laura's physical-therapy session. My parents usually came along. One day the director called me into her office. "You're doing great things with your sister. You have a lot of natural skills," she said. "You should think about becoming a physical therapist."

I laughed. "I appreciate the compliment," I said. "And the career advice. But you wouldn't think that if you knew how bad I am at science. I'm just here to help Laura."

One morning in late May, about five weeks after the accident, I mentioned to the therapist that Laura hadn't been outside. "Well, then, it's time we took her," she said. I pushed Laura's wheelchair alongside a fountain then took her hand and dipped it into the water.

"Cold," Laura said.

"That was a great idea," the therapist said. "You're helping her brain make connections again."

All the things I'd been doing in the last few weeks, strengthening Laura's hands and arms, doing small exercises for manual dexterity—it was exciting to be part of her healing. I felt a real sense of purpose. Except, it was the oddest thing. The more Laura became herself, as her ability to speak returned, as bandages were removed, somehow the less she seemed like the Laura I knew.

"Good work," the therapist said as we left the fountain. "Laura, can you thank your sister?"

"Thank you, Carly," she managed to say with some effort.

"Carly? Why did she call me that?" I asked the therapist.

"It's normal for her to be confused," she said. "Give her time."

Still, I was alarmed. Frightened. I tried not to think about it, but I couldn't get over the haunting feeling: what if this wasn't Laura?

In the next session, we sat two feet apart, tossing a beach ball back and forth. I stared intently at her face, which was still distorted by the accident, trying to match every detail against my memories of Laura. After the session, I knelt so we were eye to eye. "I want to ask you a question. Can you tell me your name?"

Slowly, with great effort, her mouth formed the word: "Whitney."

"You're doing so well," I said, squeezing her hand. My mind was racing. "What are your parents' names?"

She haltingly said, "Newell and Colleen."

Our parents were Don and Susie. She wasn't my sister.

I wheeled the young woman—suddenly a stranger—back to her room then rushed to find Mom and Dad. They were sitting on a bench down a hallway. "She's not Laura. Her name is Whitney," I gasped.

Mom and Dad said they too had begun to question whether she really was Laura. But they had been waiting to see if I shared their doubts. It all seemed so unreal and impossible. She looked so much like Laura—same blond hair, same athletic build. How could it not be her?

I slumped onto the bench, and my parents went to tell the rehab center's director our fears. All that time I'd spent with her. All that I was doing for her. *God, how could I have not known she wasn't my own sister?*

Finally, my parents returned. "Her name is Whitney Cerak. She's a freshman at Taylor," Dad said, holding my hand. "The director called the coroner's office in Indiana. Their guess is that a paramedic put Laura's purse next to Whitney on the rescue helicopter and at the hospital they assumed the ID was correct. I'm going to call the boys and ask them to meet us at home."

It hit me as I sat in the backseat of the car on the drive home: *My baby sister is dead. I'll never see Laura again.* I felt too stunned to process the information, my mind and heart on overload.

My dad pulled the car into the driveway, and there were my brothers, Mark and Kenny. For the longest time we all held each other, grief spilling over.

That night, lying in bed, I struggled to make sense of it all. *God, You have to know how much this hurts. Why would You put us through this?*

I had been wrong about so many things! God hadn't saved Laura's life. He hadn't needed me to take care of her. I hadn't been singled out for anything. It seemed such a cruel and senseless thing for our family to go through.

The next morning all I wanted to do was stay in bed. Normally I would have been in physical therapy with Laura by that time. Except it wasn't Laura—it was Whitney. Whitney's family was with her now, rejoicing in their own miracle.

The days that followed were like a whirlwind—me singing at the memorial service, more than two thousand people attending, a private burial, a constant barrage of calls from the media. The bizarre story had gone national, then global. I lived in a kind of depressed daze. The grief was less raw, but the confusion was deeper. I felt like I was emerging from my own coma, searching for my own identity.

There was only one lesson from all this that was painfully evident: life is short. I needed to find something to do, something to help me get out of bed in the morning. But what? I'd quit my job.

My mind kept circling back to what I'd lost: Laura and those physical-therapy sessions. There had to be something else. What was I missing? Then I remembered the conversation with the rehab center's director. What had she said? "You have a real gift for this, a lot of natural skill." Working with Whitney had been an amazing experience, perhaps the most fulfilling of my life. Had God been trying to tell me something? Could I actually have been where He wanted me to be all along, helping Whitney?

I needed to talk this through with someone. I grabbed my cell phone and called my best friend. "I'm thinking about going back to school to study physical therapy," I told her. "Am I crazy? You know I did awful in math and science."

"Tell me why you want to do this," my friend said.

"All I know is that I want to help other people's Lauras," I answered.

Now, months later, that was the same answer I gave to the head of the university's physical-therapy program.

She nodded. "I think there's more to it than that. Physical therapists see what's possible, beyond what the patient can sometimes envision. They help patients realize what they're capable of. Maybe that's why you're here today. You were able to help Whitney."

Last spring I graduated from the two-year program. Last May Whitney graduated too, from Taylor, on schedule. I sat in the audience as she crossed the stage to receive her diploma, a lump in my throat as I thought about all those nights I'd sat by her side. We've become good friends. After the ceremony I gave her a huge hug. "I'm so proud of you," I said. "You've come so far."

And I had too, a journey that took me from grief and tragedy to an incredible healing of my own.

By Design

When we allow God the privilege of shaping our lives, we discover new depths of purpose and meaning. What a joyful thought to realize you are a chosen vessel for God—perfectly suited for His use.

Joni Eareckson Tada

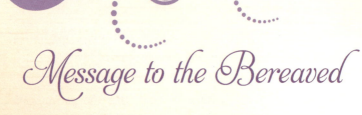

Message to the Bereaved

BY NATALIE KALMUS

D on't worry, but come to me as soon as you can," my sister Eleanor Smith wired. At the time, I was in London working out Technicolor problems with one of the British motion-picture companies.

I felt a deep, numbing pang. I knew Eleanor had been ill some time. Surely this was her gentle way of telling me the end was coming.

I could not picture—or accept it. Always radiating charm, friendliness, and an inner happiness, my sister had been a wonderful inspiration to those close to her. She had that rare trait of always giving others a pat on the back, lifting their spirits, and sending them off with a fresh outlook on life.

When first stricken by the most fearsome of medical enemies, the doctors had told her that her days were numbered. Knowing this had not made the slightest difference in her warm interest in people—nor in her deep, abiding faith in the wonder of God.

But now she needed me. I returned to the States and hurried to Eleanor, expecting to find her in bed in great pain. Instead she was in the living room perched jauntily on the sofa, looking more like a schoolgirl of seventeen than an incurably ill woman.

"Natalie." She held out her arms joyously. "I'm so happy now that you're here. We have so much to talk over." To anyone listening, I might have dropped in for a casual call.

Later, after Eleanor had retired for the night, the doctor drew me aside. "Mrs. Kalmus," he said, "I think it will be a most trying experience for you if you stay here to the end. I'm afraid that your sister's last hours will be an agony of pain."

Medically I knew he was right. Yet the exquisite radiance I noticed in my sister's face seemed to somehow refute his statement. The strange feeling swept over me that the strength of my sister's spirit could well triumph over her pain.

During the next few days I discovered that Eleanor was doing many things to baffle the doctors. They were preparing her for some very grim final moments. She ignored their solemn suggestions and remedies. One night she had me sit down on the side of her bed.

"Natalie, promise me that you won't let them give me any drugs. I realize that they are trying to help relieve my pain, but I want to be fully aware of every sensation. I am convinced that death will be a beautiful experience."

I promised. Alone later, I wept, thinking of her courage. Then as I tossed in bed on through the night, I realized that what I considered to be a calamity, my sister intended to be a triumph.

One afternoon ,Eleanor, in the most airy and lighthearted manner, asked several friends to a dinner party that she, on the spur of the moment, decided to hold. I was stunned. But Eleanor grinned at me impishly in high spirits. The sight of the happiness in her face checked my objections.

On the night of the party Eleanor dressed meticulously, concealing the pain I knew she felt. We helped her downstairs before the guests were to arrive. Sitting in a turquoise chair in her yellow evening gown, she sparkled with life and gaiety. Again I noticed the schoolgirl look on her face.

The party was a grand success; the guests were never once aware of the illness that my sister concealed so expertly. That night, however, when she was carried to bed, her deep physical weariness appeared on the surface. Then I realized that my sister knew this was her final social fling. She had planned it that way.

Ten days later the final hour drew near. I had been at her bedside for hours. We had talked about many things, and always I marveled at her quiet, sincere confidence in eternal life. Not once did the physical torture inside overcome her spiritual strength. This was something that the doctors simply hadn't taken into account.

"Dear kind God, keep my mind clear and give me peace," she had murmured over and over again during those last days.

We had talked so long that I noticed she was drifting off to sleep. I left her quietly with the nurse and retired to get some rest. A few minutes later I heard my sister's voice calling for me. Quickly I returned to her room. She was dying.

I sat on her bed and took her hand. It was on fire. Then she seemed to rise up in bed almost to a sitting position.

"Natalie," she said, "there are so many of them. There's Fred...and Ruth—what's she doing here? Oh, I know!"

An electric shock went through me. She had said Ruth! Ruth was a cousin who had died suddenly the week before. But Eleanor had not been told of Ruth's sudden death.

Chill after chill shot up and down my spine. I felt on the verge of some powerful, almost frightening knowledge. She had murmured Ruth's name.

Her voice was surprisingly clear. "It's so confusing. So many of them!" Suddenly her arms stretched out as happily as when she had welcomed me! "I'm going up," she murmured.

Then she dropped her arms around my neck—and relaxed in my arms. The will of her spirit had turned final agony into rapture.

As I laid her head back on the pillow, there was a warm, peaceful smile on her face. Her golden-brown hair lay carelessly on the pillow. I took a white flower from the vase and placed it in her hair. With her petite, trim figure, her wavy hair, the white flower, and the soft smile, she looked once more—and permanently—just like a schoolgirl.

Never again will death frighten me in any way. This was my sister's inheritance to me—her final, beautiful gift. I had seen for myself how thin was the curtain between life and death. I had glimpsed part of the wonderful truth about everlasting life.

In the weeks that followed, however, there was a tremendous vacuum inside me that I could not fill. Then, as though heaven-sent, a famous authoress came to visit me and brought me a prayer by Rudolph Steinert, written to comfort those grief-stricken by the death of loved ones.

I read the words slowly, letting them settle deep inside me. Soon many facts became clear. Without realizing it, I had been desperately trying to hold onto my sister, which was fair to neither of us. It was upsetting my own normal life. With this realization, a new peace and tranquility began to fill the emotional vacuum inside me.

A perfect relationship now exists between my sister and me. Frequently, I feel her comforting presence. At the same time I am again able to draw full satisfaction and enjoyment from both my business and social life. Whenever the opportunity arises, I am happy to share the remarkable story of my sister's passing with others for the help and comfort it can give them. And always I have the feeling that it is Eleanor herself who is passing on this beautiful understanding of death—through me.

As for those occasions when loneliness assails me, I say the words of this prayer over and over to myself as I remember them:

Into thy new surroundings let my love be woven.
Warming thy coolness, cooling thy warmness,
Live upward borne by love, illuminated by light.
The beautiful love we found
I shall now send into the realms of the spirit
To link soul with soul when, from the spirits' illuminous lands,

Thou wilt turn in search of what thou seekest in me
Thou wilt find my love in thinking.

A Beautiful Passage

Even though I walk through the valley of the
shadow of death, I will fear no evil, for you are
with me; your rod and your staff, they comfort me.

PSALM 23:4 ESV

Lasting Partnership

BY ANNE F. BEILER

E very so often, I stop by the Auntie Anne's pretzel
shop down the road from my office. These days it's
one of more than 650 stores that make and sell hand-
rolled soft pretzels using the special recipe that my husband,
Jonas, and I came up with. Yet when I breathe in that familiar,
delicious aroma of fresh-baked pretzels, it takes me back to
where my business first got off the ground—the little booth I
ran at the Downington, Pennsylvania, farmers' market twelve
years ago.

The story of Auntie Anne's, though, is about more than how
a successful international business grew from one pretzel stand.
It's about the three-decades-long partnership between Jonas and
me, the tragedy that nearly destroyed our marriage, and the work
that brought us unexpected healing.

The simple rural life of the Amish-Mennonite people was all
I knew, growing up in Lancaster County, Pennsylvania. Besides
running our farm, Mom and Dad worked at a farmers' market on
weekends. Mom was always doing something for our family—
mending our clothes, stirring a pot of stew, rolling out dough
for a pie crust, leading the eight of us kids in prayer. By the time

I was twelve, I was baking pies and cakes to sell at the market, dreaming of being a good wife and mother myself someday.

At a friend's birthday party a few years later, I was introduced to a tall young man named Jonas Beiler. He was eighteen and had a spark of humor in his eyes and a humble strength about him. I sipped my root beer and tried to act natural, but my friends noticed how he and I kept exchanging glances. "Jonas Beiler is so handsome," they teased. "We heard he likes you."

That evening someone said, "How about a game of Walk a Mile?" It's a favorite among older Amish youth, where couples hold hands and walk down the lane, changing partners each time. When my turn came to be partners with Jonas, I felt myself blushing like crazy.

Soon Jonas and I started courting. From our first date, we were so comfortable together, like we'd known each other forever. He had grown up Old Order Amish, the most conservative of the Amish-Mennonite groups, but he'd chosen not to formally join the church when he came of age. Instead of getting a horse and buggy, Jonas had pursued his fascination with cars. He bought an old junker, took it apart, and rebuilt it from the ground up, figuring out how it was put together as he went along. By the time we met, he had his own auto-repair shop. "I don't know if I can explain it," Jonas told me, "but I was just drawn to this life. It felt right for me, fixing things people depend on."

That's how I felt about Jonas. He just felt right for me.

In September 1968, we got married and moved into a trailer on his parents' farm. I ran parts for Jonas in his body shop. "It's nice to be working together, don't you think?" he'd say, coming up to the counter and taking my hand. At home, we'd stay up late into the night, holding each other and talking about everything from the children we hoped to have someday to how we both wanted a closer, more personal relationship with God.

To explore our faith, we got together with my sisters and their husbands and other young couples for prayer meetings. Out of those meetings, a new, independent church grew. Life got even better when our daughter LaWonna was born three years into our marriage. Our second child, Angela Joy, came along in January 1974. Her middle name pretty much described how I felt. Sitting in church holding Angie, with Jonas and LaWonna on either side of me, I prayed, *God, thank you for all that you've given me. To build a life, a family with the man I love...this is what I dreamed of.*

Then one September morning in 1975, that dream was shattered. We'd moved to my parents' land, and I was about to do the breakfast dishes when I noticed 20-month-old Angie scampering across the yard to see her grandma and her aunt Fi. Our daughters visited almost every morning. *Guess Angie got a head start*, I thought as I watched her disappear behind the barn. I picked up the phone to let Mom know Angie was coming.

Before I could dial, an anguished scream pierced the morning quiet. I dropped the phone and flew out the front door. My father was running toward me, Angie limp and terribly still in his arms.

"Fi was backing up the tractor..." Dad's voice cracked. "She didn't see her.... "

Angie had died instantly, the doctors later told me.

After our daughter's funeral, Jonas and I fell back on the tradition we'd been raised with—that hard work would get us through hard times. We tried to bury our grief in running the auto-repair shop and, with our dynamic new pastor's encouragement, in church activities. But no matter how much I devoted myself to church work, the doubts, the emptiness deep inside me wouldn't go away. Would our sweet Angie still be with us if I'd kept a closer watch over her? Had I failed at the job God had given me? The discovery that Jonas and I were expecting another child didn't lift me out of despair. Not even prayer seemed to help me make sense of things. *What's wrong with me?* I'd wonder to myself. *If I really have faith, I shouldn't be feeling like this.*

Jonas and I couldn't seem to talk the way we used to, couldn't bring ourselves to discuss how we felt about losing Angie. When we tried, Jonas got a sad look in his eyes. "It hurts too much to talk about it," he admitted. "Maybe we just need some time to heal our pain." But I was desperate to talk to someone. LaWonna did her best—"Don't be sad, Momma, it'll be okay," she'd say, giving me a hug—but it wasn't fair to lean on a four-year-old.

Finally I went to our pastor, Cliff [not his real name], for counseling, which in those days was unheard of for people from my background. He let me pour out my mixed-up feelings, putting his arm around me until my sobs quieted, comforting me, I thought, as I had often comforted my daughters.

Joy LaVale was born in August 1976, but our love for our new baby didn't bring Jonas and me close again. I continued to see our pastor. I thought I could trust him. He was so understanding. "Anytime you want to talk about your marriage, about anything," Cliff said, "I'm here for you, Anne."

His words—he always knew just what to say—seemed like the balm I needed for the ache in my heart. Cliff encouraged me to open up to him completely, and with my grief over Angie's death more than I could bear, I found myself telling him things I could no longer tell my husband, sharing my loneliness and deepest fears. I even confided to him that the passion in my marriage had all but flickered out.

When our church split into two groups, our family was among those who followed Cliff to Texas to start anew. Jonas found a job in an automotive business, and we threw ourselves into helping establish our new church, as if working extra-hard to build it could mask the fact that the marriage we'd built was crumbling around us.

If it weren't for the girls, Jonas and I would have hardly spoken. We barely touched. We stayed up late into the night because we were too tense to sleep with the silence hovering between us like an almost physical barrier.

Not that Jonas didn't try to reach out to me. I even noticed him reading books on psychology and family relationships, though he'd never been interested in studying anything besides cars. But I couldn't respond. I was too enmeshed in my relationship with Cliff. I knew in my heart that the emotional intimacy and intensity I shared with him should have been shared only with my husband. When I finally worked up the courage one day to express my doubts about our relationship, Cliff drew me close and asked, "Who understands you better than I do?"

Why, then, did it seem so wrong to be with him, so shameful…a betrayal of my husband's trust? Cliff's words now sounded hollow, cloying, more manipulative than comforting. Had talking with him merely numbed my pain, not healed it? Abruptly I pulled myself away from him and went home, more confused than ever.

When I saw the questions and hurt in Jonas's eyes and LaWonna's gaze dart between us, it was all I could do to keep from crying and confessing everything. But I was too ashamed to admit what I had done, too afraid that telling the truth would break up our family forever.

God was the only one who could hear me now in my shame and guilt. *I've betrayed my husband, let my daughters down. And I've betrayed You, who gave them to me to love. Please forgive me and help me do what's right.*

I pulled back from Cliff and resolved to try harder with Jonas, thinking that was enough. Then several months later, a guest counselor led a marriage seminar at our church. Afterward, Jonas came to me. "We haven't talked about this, but I wanted you to know," he said. "I spoke to the seminar leader about the problems we've had between us since Angie died."

"Jonas, wait," I choked out. "There's something you need to know." I told him everything.

At first he was too stunned to respond. "I knew something was wrong," he said eventually. "I even read books to try and figure it all out."

When Jonas suggested that we seek professional counseling, I agreed to try. For him. "For us," he said, as if he knew what I was thinking.

We saw a psychologist we knew from church. In our sessions together, Jonas and I were encouraged to share our feelings, no matter how painful, to really talk to each other for the first time in years. It was hard for me to accept that I'd been taken advantage of by our pastor, even when the truth came out that he had done the same thing to a number of women in our church who'd gone to him for advice. Harder still for me was to accept Jonas's forgiveness and to forgive myself.

"It takes two of us to make our marriage, and I didn't give you the support you needed," he said. "I don't know if we can work things out, but"—Jonas looked at me, his gaze warm and unwavering—"I know I love you and I want to try. Are you willing?"

"I'll try," I said. "But I'm afraid I might have nothing left to give." Silently I asked, *God, let me be worthy of his love.*

The more Jonas and I talked, untangling and reconciling our feelings about Angie's death and its aftermath, the more his fascination with how cars are put together was outstripped by his fascination with how people's lives are put together. He'd learned a lot from his reading and our counseling sessions, and he began taking courses toward a degree in pastoral counseling.

"I know there are Amish and Mennonite families out there who need the help we've received," Jonas said one night at dinner. "But they don't know where or how to find it. I've been thinking about starting a center where they can receive counseling for free."

The passion in his voice brought to mind the young man I'd fallen in love with. I reached across the table and took his hand, remembering the old days starting out together in his shop. "I'll help you, Jonas."

We moved back home to Pennsylvania, where Jonas did auto repair part-time. The rest of the week, he worked out of our house, counseling people from local Amish and Mennonite communities, treating their emotional needs in a spiritual context. I got a job managing a concession stand at a farmers' market in Maryland. Seeing people enjoy the food I'd made and appreciate my work, I began to believe that I wasn't a failure after all and deserved a second chance.

When a booth at the market in Downington, Pennsylvania, came up for sale, we borrowed money from Jonas's dad and bought it. I sold pizza, stromboli, ice cream, and hot, hand-rolled pretzels. The pretzels were the most popular, so I was dismayed one weekend when none of the batches I baked came out right.

I decided to try and improve them. For two months, I tinkered with the recipe, but the results were disappointing. "I'm ready to call it quits with pretzels," I told Jonas. "They look bad and taste terrible."

"Since when do we give up so easily?" he teased. "I used to help my mom with her baking sometimes. Why don't we try a little of this?" He added another ingredient to my mixing bowl. "And a little of that?" The pretzels that came out of the oven were the best we'd ever tasted!

My customers agreed. Pretty soon people weren't ordering anything else. I was selling upwards of 2,000 pretzels a day. "Something this good deserves its own special name," Jonas declared with that familiar sparkle in his eye.

In February 1988, we christened the little pretzel stand Auntie Anne's, which is what my nieces and nephews call me. In less than a year, we opened a second stand, then a third. Most importantly, we were able to put away money toward the counseling center Jonas longed to establish. People asked about running their own Auntie Anne's pretzel stands, so in 1989 I began franchising—a term I'd never heard until I started doing it!

Then came the day in 1992 when, funded by profits from our pretzels, Jonas officially opened the doors to the Family Information Center to offer free counseling to the Amish and Mennonites in the area. How amazing to see God use something as simple as a pretzel to help us realize our dreams. Today Jonas heads a staff of ten counselors at the center, treating not only those who share our background, but anyone in need.

It took many years of working through our sometimes heart-breaking struggles, but Jonas and I have succeeded in building a marriage and a life far beyond what we ever dreamed—a partnership based on the love that brought and kept us together... God's love, the truest of all.

Faith and Love

Love requires sharing,
sharing requires struggle,
struggle requires faith,
faith requires love.

Taking Time for Tenderness

BY MARY VAUGHN ARMSTRONG

I jerked on my seat belt and backed the car out of the garage, oblivious to the signs of early spring that usually gladdened my heart. I was on my way to my friend Joan's birthday breakfast, but I felt as tight as a coiled spring. My mother-in-law, Penny, had come to live with us after a series of heart problems and small strokes. And since her arrival it seemed I'd done nothing but care for her.

This morning I'd maneuvered Penny to the edge of her bed, sponged soapy water over her body, rubbed lotion into her wrinkled skin, and brushed and braided her long hair. And as I did it, I wondered: How could she just sit there and say nothing, with me working so hard? If only she'd give me one word of thanks for the total, daily care I gave her. All she said as I put a scrambled egg and whole-wheat toast in front of her was, "I wish I could have something sweet. With cinnamon. And sugar."

"Sugar's not good for you, Penny," I said, fighting to keep the tension out of my voice as I settled her into a chair by the phone and started out the door.

It wasn't fair. Penny's helplessness threatened to crowd out my simplest daily pleasures. I didn't even have time to take a break for a cup of tea, to enjoy the springtime. A dozen times a day I found myself wondering, *What about me?*

I blinked back tears as I parked the car and hurried into the restaurant. There sat my friend Joan. Her husband, Butch, had Alzheimer's disease, and she devoted herself to his care. I couldn't imagine how she kept going year after year.

"Happy birthday!" I exclaimed as Joan greeted me with a hug. When I sat down, I discovered a package at my place, wrapped in tissue paper and tied with a silver ribbon.

"Joan, what's going on? It's your birthday."

"Just open it," she urged.

Inside was a beautiful oak wall plaque. "Blessed be the God," read the gilded inscription, "who comforts us in all our affliction so that we may be able to comfort..." (2 Corinthians 1:3–4 NASB).

"Joan, it's a treasure," I whispered, awed by a friend who gave presents on her own birthday.

"I thought you could hang it where you can read it often," she said. "I discovered that verse one day, and it changed me as a caregiver."

" 'So that we may be able to comfort.' " Words quite a bit different, I thought, from "What about me?"

Joan pushed back wisps of gray hair. "When Butch got sick," she said, "all I could think of was myself. I was so tired, so guilty, so angry. But each day God always found ways to comfort me—in the touch of a friend's hand, in the beauty of the seasons, in the smallest ways. And in the same ways that God comforted me, I started searching for ways to comfort Butch."

"Like what?"

She laughed. "Nothing big there either. It turned out the littlest things made him happiest too. Like reading the comics to him, even though he doesn't understand much. Or putting a ribbon on the cat. Or popping corn and watching the news together."

I thought of Penny back home in her too-quiet room. Had I been so caught up in caring for her body that I forgot her spirit? For the first time, I tried to think of what might bring joy to her day instead of mine.

After Joan and I said good-bye, I drove to the grocery store. Near the entrance were pots of bright spring flowers, and I selected one bursting with tulips. Then I headed for the bakery and home.

"Mary?" Penny called as I opened the door. Her hands were folded in her lap on the newspaper, exactly as they'd been two hours before.

Impulsively I planted a kiss on the top of her head. "I need to take a break, Penny," I said. "How would you like to have a cup of tea together? And an apple Danish?"

Her eyes lit up. "With cinnamon...and sugar?"

"With cinnamon. And sugar. And fresh tulips!"

"It would be wonderful. Oh, Mary..."

"Yes, Penny?"

"Thank you," she said.

Tender Comfort

*You who have received so much love
share it with others. Love others the way
that God has loved you, with tenderness.*

MOTHER TERESA

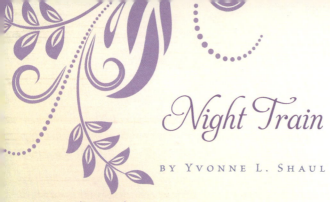

Night Train

BY YVONNE L. SHAUL

The coach swayed as the train sped westward through the winter night. I'm sure that the engineer knew his curves and inclines, but I don't think that he knew the height of my French heels, or that I was half-asleep as I groped along the darkened car. With a shriek of the whistle, the train rounded a sharp curve and I found myself on the floor, my compact and lipstick rolling down the aisle.

Angrily, I crawled along the narrow passage to recover them. Near the end of the car, I heard a woman crying.

The sounds came from the lounge, so I gently pushed open the door. The room was dark. I fumbled for the switch. The only occupant was a middle-aged woman, rocking back and forth on the seat, crying uncontrollably.

I thought she was ill, but to all offers of assistance she only shook her head. I sat beside the weeping woman, for I could not bear to leave her alone. Each time I tried to help, she began a fresh outburst of sobbing.

Finally, I told her I would go look for a doctor. The woman straightened and said quite calmly, "I'm not ill, I'm all right. I only have more trouble than I can bear."

"I'd like so much to help you."

Somehow the floodgates opened. In a rush of words that would not be held back, she told me she had lived alone in an eastern state since her husband's death some years before. Her only son was stationed in Germany with the Air Force, and her daughter had moved to California after her marriage. The daughter was dying, and it was this race to see her that the heart-broken mother was finding so difficult to bear.

What can one say to a person so stricken? What words can be of any comfort in the face of so great a sorrow?

I knew I was inadequate as I tried to recall passages from the Bible, to remember a sermon, condolences, or the usual "if it be His will," but the shaking form before me, the graying head bowed in utter despair, seemed lost to all but her own misery.

Minutes wore on. The tension mounted as steadily the wheels of the train clacked along. Then an idea came that sent me back down the aisle, peering at the sleeping passengers. I shook them awake.

Over and over I asked, "Is there a minister in this car—a priest—a rabbi?"

Finally, in desperation, I pleaded, "Who can pray? A woman needs help."

No one moved.

No one offered aid.

Suddenly, a small hand reached up from a seat and pulled at my sleeve, and a gentle voice half whispered, "Will I do? I know the Bible a little. I can pray a little too."

I looked at the child in surprise, then I took the outstretched hand and hurried back to the lounge where the grief-stricken woman sat with her head on her clasped hands.

I saw the small figure cover the woman's hands with her own, and the voice, soft with love, began to chant, "Our Father, who art in heaven...." When she reached "Thy will be done," the words took on a cadence of pure joy.

The light seemed to soften and the room to fill with a peace that I, too, could feel. I sank onto the bench and bowed my head as the child's voice took up the beautiful promise of the Twenty-Third Psalm.

Lost for a moment with my own thoughts, I was brought back to reality as the little girl began recounting the fifth chapter of Matthew. A comforting, positive "Blessed are they that mourn, for they shall be comforted" fell upon my ears.

I was surprised, then, to see that my grieving friend was sitting up, calmly. Gone was the dark despair, the defeat, the racking sobs.

At last the woman stood up. "Thank you for bringing help," she said to me. Then turning to the child between us she gently touched the little blind girl's face: "And thank you, dear, for bringing me back the comfort of my faith."

Faith in the Dark

*Often His purpose in the dark places
of our lives is to simplify our belief until our
relationship to Him is that of a child.*

CAROLYN LUNN

A Symbol of Hope

BY PRISCILLA SALYERS

I looked at the basket of yarn on the floor by my chair in the living room. It was 7:00 p.m., the end of a long day. *Can I really do this?* I wondered. Once, I'd loved knitting. I'd carried yarn and needles everywhere. I'd knitted while watching TV, standing in line at the store, even on lunch breaks from my job with the customs service in the Alfred P. Murrah Federal Building in Oklahoma City.

Then on April 19, 1995, a massive bomb blast destroyed the Murrah building. A coworker found the basket in the shell of our office, two weeks after the explosion. He brought it to my house, remembering how I was never without my knitting. It had been a tearful reunion. But later, when I took up my needles, I felt nothing. No joy. No comfort. After a few minutes I dropped the yarn into the basket. What was the point of trying to pick up where I'd left off? Nothing would ever be the same.

The basket had been sitting by my chair ever since, the skeins still covered with bits of drywall, insulation, ash. I picked up the yarn every few months, but I could never manage more than a few stitches before my mind replayed that April day. I remembered looking out my office window at the tall elm tree in the plaza, admiring its green canopy. Chatting with two of the customs agents I worked with. Then, a deafening boom, a rain of debris, followed by an even more terrifying silence. Slowly becoming aware I was alive. Being trapped in rubble for hours. Discovering afterward that 168 people had died, including the two coworkers I'd been talking to.

I'd prayed that God would help me to find comfort, some sense of meaning in my survival. But was that even possible? Two years after the bombing, I still felt a bleakness I couldn't escape. I was numb, shut off from everyone, everything, as if I were still trapped in the rubble back on that terrible morning.

Until I watched a broadcast of other Murrah victims testifying at bomber Timothy McVeigh's trial. They talked about their struggles to go on. A woman who'd lost her son told of not being able to sew anymore. A man said he no longer enjoyed woodworking. Anger surged through me. *McVeigh is stealing our joy. I can't let him do this.*

I jumped into my car and drove to the site of the Murrah building. Through the chain-link fence that still encircled the burned-out ruins, I stared angrily at the scar in the earth, the scar that was a part of me. Then I saw it. My tree. Half its branches were gone, but the elm was standing tall, almost defiantly. "If you can do it, I can do it," I whispered. I went straight to the yarn store. I knew what I wanted—no, needed—to do. For the first time in months, I felt alive again.

Now I picked up the new skein of royal-blue yarn I'd bought and snatched my needles from the basket. I pulled out a strand, hesitantly threading it between my finger and thumb. Once, just feeling the softness of the yarn would've been enough to set my hands in motion. I'd done some beautiful work. I'd made sweaters that sold for hundreds of dollars. But the real payoff was the joy I felt inside, the kind of deep, satisfying joy that makes you feel connected to God. Could I rekindle that passion? I made a loop from the blue yarn and slipped it over a needle, pulling the yarn tight. I made another loop, casting on again. Over and over I cast on, sliding the knots down my needle, counting as I went. Ten knots. Twenty. Thirty. It dawned on me that I'd long passed the point where I usually had to stop. My fingers were nimbly working, as if someone were directing them.

Knots ran the length of a needle, nearly eighty; I began stitching the ribbing for a border across the bottom of a sweater. I thought about all the people who'd died. So many lives cut short. I looked at my basket and saw a skein of red yarn, blackened in parts, covered with ash. Red...red hearts. What if I knitted 168 hearts into the border of the sweater? It would be a memorial only I could create. The debris-littered skeins were tangible reminders of the darkest day of my life. And yet I could see purpose in intertwining new yarn with the old, a bridge between my grief and a future only God could see.

I picked up the red yarn and looped a strand around a needle. A row of hearts spread across the bottom of the sweater, then another above that. With each stitch it felt as if I were reclaiming part of my life. I was doing something that mattered. I was knitting a victory sweater.

I looked over at the clock. I'd knitted for more than three hours! The back of a sweater, six inches deep, lay on my lap. I counted the hearts: 44. It was a start. There'd be more knitting, and more healing, ahead. I pictured what I'd add to the sweater to honor my coworkers and the others lost that day: the chain-link fence, mementos left by mourners. And, of course, my tree, with its new leaves of spring. A symbol of survival and, like my sweater, of hope.

Reason to Hope

"For I know the plans I have for you," declares the LORD, *"plans to prosper you and not to harm you, plans to give you hope and a future."*

JEREMIAH 29:11 NIV

Chance Encounter

BY JANET HERSHBERGER

I was a bit uneasy when I couldn't reach Heidi on the phone that snowy day in March. But I'd long since gotten used to being anxious when it came to my twenty-four-year-old daughter. Over the previous six years Heidi had disappeared repeatedly, without explanation. During that same period she'd had four children out of wedlock, each father out of her life before the baby was even born. But the last few months it had seemed she was finally coming around, holding a steady job at the Greencroft retirement home, taking care of her newborn twins, coming to church with my husband Jerry and me on Sundays.

The snow was coming down fast as I headed down the main hallway of Parkside Elementary after grading some papers, so it took me a moment to make out the two figures approaching the door. Policemen. "We're looking for Janet Hershberger," one of them said.

"I'm Janet Hershberger," I said, holding the door open.

"Is there a private place we can talk?" he asked quietly. And that's when I knew, even before we went inside and they sat me down in an empty classroom, telling me how Heidi had lost control of her car on a slippery road and careened into oncoming traffic. The fear that had haunted me all those long, restless nights when I didn't know where Heidi was had become reality. Heidi was never coming home again.

I wished I could turn back the years to shortly after Jerry and I adopted Heidi and her brother J.D., when the two of them clung fast to my hands as we stood in that very spot just inside the door before school, Heidi's pretty green eyes turned up to me eagerly as I admired her latest crayon drawing. I never dreamed that one day those eyes would cloud over with troubled secrets, that I would search them for a clue as to what was going on in my daughter's head, that Heidi would become more of a mystery to me than the impossible-seeming jigsaw puzzles she spent countless hours putting together.

The policemen drove me to the hospital, where one of Heidi's twins, Jasmine, was in critical condition. I closed my eyes and prayed, just as I had so many times since Heidi first disappeared the night before her final exams, senior year. We'd called her friends from church. No one had seen her. We'd called the police, then Jerry and I held each other on the living room couch, asking God to wrap His arms around our daughter and keep her safe.

She'd come home the next morning as if nothing had happened. "What were you thinking, Heidi?" I demanded. "Do you have any idea how worried we were? Don't you realize how disrespectful it is to not even pick up the phone and tell us you're okay?" Heidi didn't apologize, just sat stony-faced, answering in monosyllables, until finally tramping upstairs to her room.

It happened again that summer, but that time she vanished for two agonizing weeks. Jerry and I thought a change of scene might be the answer. We sent her to stay with family friends in Minnesota.

"Mom, please forgive me for the way I acted," she told me over the phone. But soon after returning home she took off again. One month passed, then two. The police couldn't do much because she was over eighteen. I checked with her friends from her youth group, but the problem was Heidi had other friends, ones she kept hidden from us. The unfinished jigsaw puzzle in her room was a continual reminder of her sudden absence and our frustrated attempts to figure out where she was or indeed who she was.

God, just give me a clue to help me find my daughter. One day I reached into my jacket pocket and pulled out a phone number I didn't recognize. Curious, I called it. To my amazement, Heidi answered. My joy was cut short when she said, "Mom, I have to tell you something. I'm pregnant."

We encouraged her in the decision to put the child up for adoption. She went off to college. But there she ended up in an abusive relationship, and it resulted in another child, Joana. Jerry and I eventually took Joana into our home because Heidi's behavior was too unpredictable. We suspected drugs or sexual addiction but never knew for sure the cause of Heidi's actions. Over and over she tried to get back on track, returning home and to church. I'd slip into her room in the mornings and watch her sleeping, so innocent, so peaceful. But when she awoke I always saw turmoil in her eyes, some secret life that caused her to run off again and again.

Whether we were harsh or forgiving, confrontational or gentle, nothing Jerry and I said or did seemed to get through to her. In the end all I could do was pray—during the solitude of my morning devotions, in the fellowship of our church group, or at bedtime with Jerry, the plea was always the same: *Lord, please give Heidi Your protection and peace. Guide her back to You.*

I thought maybe, just maybe, those prayers were finally being answered when Heidi moved in with two girls from church and took a job at a local retirement home. But then a letter in the mailbox the day after Christmas 2000 brought the news that she was about to deliver twins. Reeling, I went to the hospital to see her shortly after they were born. "I'm going to take care of them myself," Heidi told me. "I have the job at the home now, and I'm going to stick with it. I'm going to move in with a really nice older couple. No more drama, I promise."

Just two months later I arrived at the hospital to learn that one of the twins, Joseph, had come through the car accident without a scratch, but Jasmine's skull had been crushed. She was being kept alive by a respirator. I found Jerry and we wordlessly embraced. Pastor Layman from our church approached me. "I just wanted you to know that Heidi was in my office yesterday, and we had the most wonderful conversation. There is no doubt in my mind that Heidi is with the Lord."

I felt an immense calm settle over me, and his words resounded in my mind: "Heidi is with the Lord." That assurance stayed with me while I held our tiny granddaughter, Jasmine, as she took her last breath. I imagined I was handing her over to Heidi.

That's how we buried them, mother and child together. Hundreds of friends and relatives came to the funeral. Even some of the residents of the retirement home where Heidi worked showed up. After all the times Heidi had left without a good-bye, it was healing for me to be able to bid her one at last.

And what a blessing to come home not to silence but to the sounds of our grandchildren! Heidi and J.D. had been toddlers when we'd adopted them, so caring for two-month-old Joseph was a newfound joy. Jerry and I surrounded ourselves with mementos from Heidi's life so the children would grow up knowing their mother.

We talked about her often. It's strange, but Heidi's presence in death seemed larger than when she was alive but always missing. Her old clothes and shoes, the tea party dishes she used to play with, her senior picture on the wall, even Joseph's smile and Joana's laugh—all brought to mind my daughter. But gone was the fear that used to darken every thought of her.

"Don't you feel angry that it ended like this after everything you went through?" my friends asked. But the calm that had come over me in the hospital was still with me. Even though I missed Heidi, there was no anger, no crushing sorrow. *How can*

I be so calm, Lord? I prayed. *Shouldn't I be grieving more for my daughter?* How could I have tossed and turned so many nights over Heidi while she was alive, yet now feel such peace when I thought of her? And then the answer came, as clearly as if Jesus were speaking to me. *You've been grieving for her for six years. She's safe with Me now.*

The cards and visits from friends subsided as the months passed. But one afternoon a couple came to call. They were the ones Heidi had been staying with at the time of her death. "Heidi was halfway through this when she died," the woman said, presenting me with a jigsaw puzzle depicting a wintry holiday scene. "There was a piece missing, but we finished the rest and thought you'd like to have it." I thanked them, but after they left, my eye was drawn to the empty spot in the puzzle. *So like Heidi*, I thought. Always a piece we didn't see. The good girl doing her homework, playing on the soccer team, going to church on the one hand. And on the other...elusive, troubled, unknowable.

Staring at the puzzle, I was suddenly right back in the midst of the doubts that had besieged me while Heidi was alive. What if she'd just been deceiving us all, telling Pastor Layman and me what she thought we wanted to hear? What if she was as troubled in death as she was in life?

My fears nagged at me, though I told no one about them except God. They were soon pushed aside, however, by an unexpected invitation. The composer of some music we'd used at Heidi's funeral offered to fly me to Nashville to talk about Heidi and how the music had comforted us. I'd never flown alone before and was more than a little nervous about it. But Jerry thought it would be good for me to get away for a few days.

South Bend Airport was daunting enough—I didn't know how I'd manage my connecting flight at bustling Detroit Metro. *Lord, please send someone to help me find my way.* The person sitting closest to me at the gate was a lovely white-haired woman who didn't look any more worldly than I. Still, I felt drawn to speak to her. "Where are you headed?"

"Nashville, Tennessee," she said with a smile. I introduced myself and learned her name was Luba. Since she was also flying to Nashville and nervous about flying by herself, we agreed to help each other find the right connecting plane when we landed at Metro.

In Detroit, despite the crowds of strangers hurrying to make their flights, porters pushing luggage carts, and bewildering signs and monitors, I felt so at ease with Luba at my side.

"So what brings you to Nashville?" she asked as we walked toward our gate. Oddly, I didn't feel the slightest awkwardness telling her about my daughter's death. "It feels so natural to talk to you about Heidi," I said.

Luba stopped suddenly, then turned to look right at me. "Heidi? Heidi Hershberger? You're Heidi Hershberger's mother?" I nodded. "My sister knew your daughter!"

Knew Heidi? In the middle of the rushing crowd, I was aware of nothing except Luba as she shared her story of Heidi. Her sister had been visiting a friend whom Heidi was looking after at the Greencroft retirement home. "She said she was really impressed by how caring Heidi was. So she started talking with her. Heidi told her she'd lived a troubled life but had made things right with God. Later we were shocked to read about the accident in the paper but heartened because we knew Heidi is with the Lord."

It took a moment to sink in, for me to make sense of it all. Then I reached out and embraced Luba. *Heidi is with the Lord.* Pastor Layman had said it, I had felt it in my heart, but it was through an unlikely meeting with a kind stranger that I was given the final assurance that my daughter had found the piece that was missing in her life. At last she was home to stay.

Lasting Peace

*God takes life's pieces and
gives us unbroken peace.*

GOUGH

Out of My Control

BY BRADLEE E. WEBBER

Numb with worry, I sped down the freeway toward the hospital where rescue units had taken my three kids. "I was afraid that trip was a mistake from the beginning," I exploded to my wife, Kim. "That's a twenty-one-hour drive each way." I let off steam so I wouldn't have to think about how badly hurt the kids might be. The camper had lost a wheel and flipped on the freeway just a half hour short of home.

I had tried to tell my ex-wife, Debbie, that the trip wasn't a good idea. But since the divorce I hadn't had any say about what happened to the kids. I had to depend on Debbie to make responsible decisions. She, her sister, and their mother were driving our three kids and their two cousins from Portland to Disneyland and back, and there wasn't a thing I could do about it. Now, my worst fears had come to pass. Not only did I not have control, I might have lost them altogether.

At the hospital, we found my eight-year-old son, Aaron, in the emergency room, surrounded by doctors who worked to keep him breathing. His face was bloody and swollen, and he had a breathing tube in his mouth.

"Aaron, it's Dad. Can you hear me?" I took hold of his hand. "You are going to be okay. The doctors will fix you up. Do you understand?" He squeezed my hand. "I'll be here when you wake up. I love you," I said. And the orderlies wheeled him away to surgery. I felt helpless. I had to trust.

The nurse told me that Jason, my 16-year-old, had suffered only minor bumps and bruises, and my ex-wife had been admitted. But meanwhile, five-year-old Jesseca was in the intensive care unit. The doctor there told us a CAT scan had revealed a bad concussion. The pressure on her brain could be fatal, and they were considering a skull tap to relieve it. I felt sick; this was a nightmare.

After three hours in intensive care, I needed to go and check on Aaron. Jesse begged me not to go. I stayed with her until she fell asleep around 10:00 p.m. The nurse told us that Jesse would be woken up every half hour so she wouldn't slip into a coma. "You go to Aaron and I'll stay with her," Kim said.

I let my mom know what was happening, then I dialed my good friend Mike Teeters. Mike and I had worked together as mechanics for TRI-MET, the bus system in Portland. He had gotten me interested in searching the Scriptures for answers to life's problems. I needed to talk to him now. I told him what had happened and said, "Will you pray for them?"

"I'll meet you there," Mike said.

Alone now for a few minutes, I wrestled with my faith. How could God let this happen? I felt angry at Him. I wanted my kids to live, to be perfect again. That was my will. But I knew it was out of my control. What was God's will?

I knew that sometimes God says no. Some children die, even though the parents pray as hard as they can. Who was I to expect any special favors from God? I tried to prepare myself to accept His will, if it should be different from mine.

Soon Mike came through the door and hugged me. I told him that Aaron was still in surgery after five and a half hours. Together we walked to a vast lobby, where Kim's parents were waiting. Kim's mother said she had phoned their church's prayer chain.

"I think we should pray now," Mike said. We formed a circle and held hands. Then we took turns praying aloud. We acknowledged God's presence—where two or more are gathered in His name, as the Bible says. Someone asked God to comfort me, and I did feel comforted. We prayed for the doctors' wisdom, skills, and hands, but most of all for Aaron and Jesseca to be restored to health. Mike wrapped it up by saying, "We surrender the children to Your loving care, Lord. They're in Your hands."

I felt encouraged. If God wouldn't listen to me, surely He would listen to these people who seemed closer to Him. When my own faith faltered, I hung onto theirs. I began to allow myself to count on Him to come through for me.

The surgeons, dressed in pale green with tight-fitting green caps, came from the operating room. White surgical masks hung from their necks. We shook hands and they sat down across from us at a low round table. "We feel pleased that we've been able to pretty well reconstruct his face," one surgeon said. He went on to explain in detail how they had handled each of the broken bones in Aaron's face. He said Aaron would temporarily be unable to speak because of the tracheotomy.

"Will he look the same?" Kim's mother asked the question I had been afraid to ask. Everyone had always said he looked like me.

"There's no way to predict. Really, I think he'll look normal once the swelling goes down, but no, he won't look exactly the same as he did. There's just no way. Remember, he is very lucky to be alive."

I shook the doctors' hands. I'd heard enough. "Thank you, doctors. I appreciate it," I said. "I know you've done your best."

I heard the words, the polite phrases, but I felt anger rising up again. Yes, thank God he's alive, but he'll never look the same. Never be the same. Sure, it could have been worse—but it also could have been better. It could have not happened at all! I had to force myself to focus on my gratitude to God for sparing Aaron's life.

But I felt like screaming at Debbie. Why hadn't she listened to me? Deep down I knew it wasn't all her fault. I struggled to control my feelings.

Next I was blaming myself. Since the divorce I'd had no control. A father should be able to keep things like this from happening, and I hadn't. I fought to keep from breaking down as I went upstairs to be with Aaron when he woke up. I had promised him. I could control that.

Aaron's face was still swollen and he was breathing through a tube. I knew he hurt; a single tear trickled down his cheek. He pointed to his mouth, and I gave him a sip of water. Then I stayed the rest of the night with him.

By 5:00 a.m. I was dead tired, but I wanted to check on Jesse. Aaron tried to hold onto my hand, tried to keep me from leaving. I assured him I'd be right back. When I reached Jesse, I found they had taken a second CAT scan. The hemorrhaging had stopped and the mass of fluid in her skull had dissipated! The doctor said that almost never happens with such a large mass, adding, "I don't know where it went, but it's gone. She's laughing!"

The nurse said it was amazing to view the two scans. "You wouldn't believe it was the same little girl!" But I believed it; after all, there were at least four prayer chains going. I knew God had heard us.

When I returned to Aaron, I took a marker board and pen so that he could communicate with me. I also took along some pictures of him in his Little League uniform. I wanted him to imagine himself well and playing ball again.

The first things Aaron wrote on his board were "Where's Mom?" and "How is Jesse?" Of course! In my anxiety about protecting him from any news that would worry him, I had neglected to let him know that everyone was alive. I was grateful that all the news was relatively good. He was the worst injured.

After they released Jesseca, we were told Aaron would have to undergo more surgery to remove some packing and to put in a smaller breathing tube. He looked scared when I told him, but

I explained that he might be able to talk after the operation. The new tube would be small enough that he could cover the opening and get air up through his throat.

The next morning I waited in a small, semidarkened family area near the operating room. His mother was still hospitalized. I would see him through this. It hurt to send him back into surgery after what he'd already been through. I paced like a caged animal for an hour and a half.

"Mr. Webber?" The surgeon appeared in the doorway. "The operation went well. Aaron would like to see you."

I stepped into the hall just as they pushed Aaron through the double doors of surgery. I bent over the gurney and ran my fingers through his straight blond hair, just the way I used to do to put him to sleep when he was a baby.

"How ya doin', little buddy?"

He covered the opening in the tube with his small fingers. "I can talk now," he croaked, smiling as best he could. Then he whispered, "I love you, Dad."

To hear him speak at all was music to my ears, but to have that be the first thing he wanted to say was more than I could handle. I just lost it. I let go and cried.

And in that moment, all the anger, all the frustration simply disappeared. *Thank You, Lord*, I prayed, *thank You.*

I saw now that I really didn't have to be in control of my kids. They were in His hands, as Mike had said. Where I was powerless, God was powerful. I had to turn it all over to Him. I had no choice. Anger wasn't doing me any good, and it certainly wasn't helping the kids.

As I let go of the anger I felt more open to God's will than ever before. Silently I asked Him what He wanted me to do, how I could help my kids. The answer, I thought I heard Him say, was, *"Just love them, no matter what."*

The accident brought things into focus for me. At the time when the kids needed me most, the only thing I had to give them was love. And that's the way it will have to be from now on. My discipline over my kids and most of my time with them are gone. But I'll always have the power to love them. Love is the most powerful force of all. And that is certainly in my control.

The Power of Love

Help me to love, Lord,
not to waste my powers of love,
to love myself less and less in order
to love others more and more.

MICHAEL QUOIST

My Computer Prayer

BY LOIS LONNQUIST

There I sat, at the end of a long, hot day in August, staring dejectedly at the computer screen. I was surrounded by stacks of bills to pay and commercials to write for our four-month-old radio station in Great Falls, Montana. My dinner was getting cold at my desk, not far from the sofa I used for catnaps. Too often my office was also my bedroom and dining room. My husband, Del, and I were working seven days a week. What had we got ourselves into?

Del had told me his plan six months earlier. Our six children were grown and we had sold our two radio stations in the Midwest. He wanted to try something new, he said, although he admitted there was some risk.

We would buy a failed, off-the-air station a thousand miles away, near Great Falls, and put it back on the air with a new format: big band music from the '30s and '40s, which we would get from a satellite feed. Our son Roger would become our engineer. The station would soon pay for itself, Del felt, and until it did, our costs would be covered by payments from the new owners of our Midwest stations.

Although I had my reservations, it seemed like a good idea. We had 25 years of experience in radio. Together, Del and I prayed for guidance, and in March we put our home up for sale and made our move.

We found a weathered one-story building surrounded by knee-deep weeds and prairie grass. A chilly March wind whistled through a 240-foot transmission tower greatly in need of paint. "We're going to love it here!" Del burst out. After he pried off some boards with a hammer, we climbed in through a porch window for our first glimpse of the dusty microphones and turntables.

It took three weeks to repair equipment, install new control boards and recorders, set up the satellite dish, and scrub every inch of the building's interior. By mid-April KXGF-AM was on the air.

Listeners loved the format. But many advertisers were wary, waiting for us to prove ourselves where others had failed. Payments from the Midwest stations were slow in coming. Short of revenue, we found ourselves living, eating, and sleeping at the station in order to keep it on the air 24 hours a day, seven days a week.

By August, I desperately needed some time off. So, sitting there at my computer, I typed, "Dear God, why are we doing this? We are almost broke. We are exhausted. How long can we go on?" Then I held down the question-mark key and watched *??????????* *???????????????????????* zoom across the screen.

I went into the control room for a commercial and station break, then walked out onto the porch. The western sky was on fire with a glorious red-and-gold sunset. Inside, a network announcer was introducing "A String of Pearls."

The next morning I sorted through the usual variety of bills and fan letters. The last one I opened was neatly written on pale blue stationery.

"Dear Friends at KXGF," it began. "I am writing to thank you for your station and the beautiful music you play. My wife and I have been faithful listeners ever since you went on the air. We've been so happy to hear the old familiar tunes.

"Two months ago my wife became ill. Many times she was awake all night in great pain. Your station was our constant companion; music soothed her suffering. When she had to go to the hospital, we took a radio along.

"Early this morning your announcer played 'I'll Be Seeing You,' our favorite song. My wife looked at me and smiled. A short time later she passed away."

Tears filled my eyes as I leaned back in my chair and looked out at the mountains. I thought about our many listeners, especially the lonely ones who couldn't sleep, or who traveled or worked at night. The letter reminded me that God had not forgotten us. Just as our music had comforted that man and his wife, I felt comforted and restored.

As it turned out, several months later we were offered a good price for the station and recouped our investment. That was ten years ago. We went on to build two more stations. KXGF is still on the air, playing the same big-band music, and we often tune in. Of the five radio stations we've built, it is our favorite. And of the many prayers we've said over those stations, my computer prayer is still the most memorable—the one whose answer I will never forget.

Comforting Notes

I wish you love, and strength,
and faith, and wisdom,
goods, gold enough to help
some needy one.
I wish you songs,
but also blessed silence,
And God's sweet peace
when every day is done.

DOROTHY MCDONALD

"I Know You're Alone"

BY ELISSA FRY KAUPISCH

The whisper on the telephone was harsh, menacing: "I know you're alone."

I slammed down the receiver, but the caller's words rang over and over in my mind. For months I'd been harassed by this anonymous caller, and now he was becoming bolder.

Was he involved in the recent rash of local burglaries? How could I possibly protect myself if someone tried to break in? As a newly divorced woman living alone with my five-year-old son, Andy, I felt completely vulnerable.

Four years earlier my husband and I had moved back to our hometown, hoping that life near our families would draw us closer together and save our marriage. But during the third year, we divorced. To support myself, I took a job teaching at the local high school. Soon afterward the calls began.

The police told me to ignore them, that the caller would soon tire of the game and quit. Several weeks passed, but the calls continued. I thought about getting an unlisted number. But with my mother's poor health and my dad on the road so much, I was afraid someone wouldn't be able to reach me in an emergency.

Finally I discussed the situation with my friend Sherry at school. "It might be one of my students," I said. "The voice is unnaturally low, like a young man trying to sound older."

I couldn't let myself verbalize the fear that a burglar was checking to see if I was home.

"Can't the phone company trace the calls?" Sherry asked.

"I'll find out today," I said just as the bell rang for the start of school.

During my break I called the phone company. "We don't have time to trace every prank call," the customer service representative said.

My mind was not on teaching the rest of the day. I scrutinized each male student's face. But not one revealed the slightest sign of guilt.

That evening I sat with my son, watching TV and wondering when the caller would phone again. Looking down at Andy snuggled close in my arms, I wished I felt as safe as he.

Later, as we headed for bed, I bolted and chained both exterior doors and shoved a kitchen chair in front of each. I tried to fall asleep, but the words replayed in my mind: "*I know you're alone.*"

I wondered, *Where are You in all this, God? Don't You care what happens to me?*

I had scarcely drifted off to sleep when I was awakened by Andy's cries.

I found him sobbing in his room. "Mommy, I'm scared," he said. "I'm afraid something will happen to you and I'll be all alone."

I climbed into bed next to him and held his hand. Light from the street lamp filtered through the curtains. "Don't be afraid," I said, stroking his silky blond hair. "You're not alone. Mommy loves you, and I'll always be here with you."

Funny, it was so simple and natural to comfort my son, but I didn't know how to calm my own fears.

A week later, around midnight, I awoke to tapping at my bedroom window. I sprang upright in bed. Did I really hear something? After several minutes I lay back down, trying to convince myself it was only a dream.

But then I heard tapping at the other window, louder this time. I held my breath. My heart pounded. I sat perfectly still... listening, waiting.

Gravel crunched in the alley. A branch snapped. I gasped as something brushed against the house. I heard muffled voices.

Leaving the lights off, I went into my bathroom and peeked out a corner of the window. Shadows shifted just beyond the alley light.

I crept to the phone and dialed the police. "I've got prowlers outside my house!"

"Give me your name and address," came the response. No sooner had the words left my mouth than the woman said, "Oh, it's you again."

"Please hurry," I pleaded.

"Yeah...we'll send a squad car as soon as one's available."

I stood in the shadows near my front window, waiting. Forty-five minutes later a patrol car cruised by slowly, its spotlight sweeping the house. Then it sped away. A half hour passed. An hour. The squad car never returned, but neither did the troublemakers.

Now I was like a frightened rabbit, jumping at every noise. I left lights, radios, and the television on all night and buttressed the doors with heavier furniture.

But the more I barricaded myself, the more victimized I felt. One night it dawned on me that the situation was getting out of hand. My dark imaginings, like my son's, were worse than reality.

I thought about my mother and how she had taught me that God loves me and watches over me. She had always told me the Bible gave her comfort and strength. Now I wondered, *Is there really something to it?* I began to search the Scriptures for myself.

Over the next several days I discovered dozens of passages related to courage and fear. One that became especially meaningful was Joshua 1:9: "Have I not commanded you? Be strong and courageous. Do not be afraid; do not be discouraged, for the LORD your God will be with you wherever you go" (NIV).

I committed that verse to memory. Each night as I recited the words, I envisioned God standing beside my bed comforting me, just as I comforted my son.

The troublesome phone calls continued. But as God's peace began to take hold of me, my fears subsided.

Then one day Sherry stopped me as I walked down the hall to my classroom. "Have you heard? One of the English teachers received some harassing calls too, and she recognized the voice as one of her students. She confronted him yesterday after school. He confessed everything—even to calling you and tapping on your windows."

"Really? What's going to happen to him?" I asked.

"He's never been in trouble before. She thinks he was just pulling a prank but should be taught a lesson nonetheless. She promised she wouldn't turn him in to the police if he would agree to tell his parents and then present written proof that he was receiving counseling. He was so worried that he would have agreed to almost anything. I'm sure you feel relieved."

Yes, I thought, *but not for the reason you think.* Sure, I was glad he'd been caught. But most of all, I had found relief from my fears. In seeking God, I had found peace. And I had begun to hear a different voice, stronger than the one on the phone, saying, *"You are not alone."*

God with Us

God walks with us. He scoops us up
in His arms or simply sits with us
in silent strength until we cannot avoid
the awesome recognition that yes,
even now, He is there.

GLORIA GAITHER

All I Ever Wanted

BY ELIZABETH SWAYNE

I was sitting in the home of a friend the other day, planning a church youth program. The floor of the home was earth, the roof grass, the kitchen a fire in front of the door. And I thought again, as I have so often during my ten years in Africa, how strange it was that I should be here. I was the girl who loved dancing and champagne and fast cars. What had happened to me?

My mind went back, as it always does, to that September day twelve years before when I was sitting in a very different kind of home in England and heard the phone ring. I almost didn't answer it. It couldn't be my husband, Ian, and if it wasn't Ian then it didn't matter. Ian and I had been married eight years, during which time no one else and nothing else had mattered.

Coming to England with him had meant leaving behind my family and friends in Indiana—I hadn't cared. I had few friends in England; we had no children, and Ian was all I'd ever wanted—Ian, who meant laughter and love and adventure.

We had one rule: we would never phone each other. Ian was a test pilot. I knew that if I started waiting for a phone call, I would be listening for it every second, imagining it was late, building every moment into a disaster.

And that is why I almost didn't pick up the phone that afternoon. When at last I did, it was to hear the nonsensical words: "I'm so very, very sorry. There's been an accident."

I almost smiled. "Ian's not flying today," I said. "I put him on the train to Glasgow this morning."

The voice pressed on, unhearing. "Ian never knew it. He was killed instantly."

"He's not flying," I pleaded. "He's on the train."

"Yes, he was in the car that jumped the rail."

I don't know how long it took me to understand that there had been a train wreck. Ian's mother and father made all the arrangements for the funeral down at the family home in Hampshire. They wanted me to come live with them there, but I knew I had to stay close to where Ian and I had been together.

I moved into a small apartment and went on with the only activity I knew: living for Ian. I decorated the rooms in his favorite colors, cooked the meals he liked, and knew I must find some other answer or go crazy.

"Keeping busy," I had heard, helped people like me. I took a secretarial job for a couple of months and then quit.

"Find someone who needs you," was another formula I clutched at. There was a nursing home in Woking: I volunteered to take a few of them out driving, but they knew and I knew that I was only going through the motions.

I realized that a lot of bereaved people became "religious." Although I had never been a churchgoer, there was a small chapel nearby that I visited. The minister invited me to the adult confirmation class. I attended faithfully, memorized long verses, and was confirmed along with the rest of the class. It meant nothing.

I had tried my best. There was nothing else I knew to do.

And it was at this point that strange and inexplicable events began to occur.

One afternoon, while walking Ian's dogs, I happened to pass the entrance to a small woodworking factory. To this day I do not understand why I turned in at the gate and asked for a job. Almost as though I had been expected, they told me to report to the front office on Monday.

My assignments were routine, but unlike my previous typing job I thoroughly enjoyed them. The work-a-day noises coming from the factory had a purposeful sound. Keeping pretty much to myself, I barely noticed the pale, worried-looking girl—Joyce something-or-other—whose desk was near my own.

Late one afternoon, I was startled by the sound of sobbing nearby. Joyce looked up, ashamed, confused, her eyes asking what she could not put into words. *"Talk to me...."*

"Come have tea at my apartment," I suggested.

While I put on the kettle, Joyce blurted out her story. Four months ago she'd had a baby in a home for unwed mothers. This week she'd signed the final adoption papers that took him away forever. Her own family, she said, had turned her out when she became pregnant. "The baby was everything I had in the world!"

And so began my deep involvement in Joyce's life. I spent every spare hour walking and talking with her, trying to fill the ache inside her. Only one part of her life I did not share. Through the doctor who'd delivered her baby, she had been introduced to a prayer group that met every Wednesday evening. Each week she would beg me to go with her, and each week I'd find a different excuse.

At last, so as not to hurt her feelings, I agreed to go "just once."

Five weeks passed and I had not missed a single Wednesday evening. How different from the confirmation class that had been weekly drudgery—I counted the days now by how far they were from Wednesday. On that unforgettable sixth time we were reading aloud from the Gospel of John. In my Bible, so new the pages still stuck together, I followed the story of the woman of Samaria who met Jesus at Jacob's well. A chill went through me. It was as if the story were not about a woman who lived two thousand years ago, but about me.

Here was a woman who was as much a stranger to Jesus as I was, who no more expected Him to turn and speak to her than I did. She'd been coming to the well day in, day out—always ending up just as thirsty as before. How this reminded me of those dry months spent trying to "keep busy" and "help others" and "find religion."

But this woman did meet Jesus. What a shock it must have been to her to learn that He knew all about her past, all her failures. More than that, He offered the answer.

" 'If you knew the gift of God...you would have asked Him, and He would have given you living water.... Everyone who drinks of this water will thirst again, but whoever drinks of the water that I will give him shall never suffer thirst" (John 4:10, 13–14 NASB).

Was He offering me this water too? Had He known me all along as He knew her? Had He been the one who led me to Joyce, when by myself I had found no one who needed me? This relationship was changing now. In the weeks since she had joined the prayer group, Joyce had been less dependent on me. She had found something better. Was He offering me, too, this better thing?

In a kind of daze I began to learn all I could about the Christian life. I read books, I asked questions, I attended conferences, and at one of these I met the director for East Africa of the Church Missionary Society (CMS). "Have you ever thought of becoming a missionary?" he asked me.

A missionary! The very word sent chills of horror through me, along with images of sensible shoes, hair buns, and cotton stockings. But could this be Christ offering me a drink of living water again?

I went to talk with the CMS board in London, almost hoping they would turn me down. But a few days later came a letter: I was to report to the missionary training college.

I arrived with my golf clubs in the backseat, three evening dresses in the trunk. At the end of the course I left for Africa, still convinced they had the wrong person for the job.

My first assignment only confirmed the feeling: it was to a refugee camp in central Kenya for women widowed in the Mau

Mau emergency. *What in the world,* I thought desperately, *do I have to say to victims of such tragedy?*

And suddenly I knew that I had everything to say to them. Wasn't I a widow? Couldn't I simply tell them the truth, that Christ had met me at my point of need and would meet them there too?

That was ten years ago and every assignment since then, whether teaching or typing, youth work or driving a truck, has been the same. I've started out feeling helpless; I've looked back to know that I both gave and received something needful.

It's true that the golf clubs are rusty, the evening dresses are gathering dust, but it's a wonderful life. Adventure, love, and laughter, all I ever wanted, have been mine since a Wednesday night long ago when I made the first prayer of my life.

"Lord," I whispered, "give me a drink of that water, that I may never be thirsty again."

Living Water

From God, great and small, rich and poor, draw living water from a living spring, and those who serve Him freely and gladly will receive grace answering to grace.

THOMAS À KEMPIS

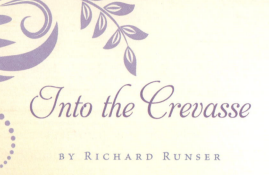

Into the Crevasse

BY RICHARD RUNSER

The ice was as smooth as glass that March day as I drove my snow machine over the Nelchina Glacier in Alaska. The vast stretches of untouched snow, the distant powder-white peaks of the Chugach Mountains, the endless blue sky—this long-awaited trip from Eureka Lodge to Valdez was turning out to be everything I'd hoped for and more, a close-up look at one of God's most-stunning canvases.

Yet it was clouded by anxiety I couldn't explain. I'd called my wife, Marge, that morning before I set out with the ten other drivers promising I'd phone again after we reached Valdez. Normally, Marge would be with me on a trip like this. Both in our fifties and longtime snow machiners, when we'd married we'd decided to explore the Alaskan wilderness together. Then we retired from our teaching careers and stepped up our expeditions, sometimes trekking the tundra for as long as two weeks at a time. Our children (from previous marriages) were grown and on their own, so it was just the two of us and the pure beauty of the ice. Those had been some of our favorite times. *Maybe I'm just missing Marge*, I decided, dismissing my unease.

This trip over the glaciers to Valdez was one we both wanted to take but had put off because we were unfamiliar with the trail. Then my son-in-law, Herb Bond, told me he had organized a group to make the journey, most of whom had done the route before. Unfortunately, Marge was going to be with her daughter in Seattle that weekend. "Don't miss it because of me," she'd urged. "It'll be breathtaking."

And it was. No trees, no animals, just mile upon mile of gently rolling ice hills. We drove over frozen rivers, passed by gaping crevasses, with no sound but the hum of our engines. I tried to clear my mind of everything but the beauty surrounding me.

By midday we were about halfway to Valdez. The group had scattered a bit, but I was still going by the book, following in the tracks of the machine in front of me, which was driven by a fellow named Clark Perry. Herb was behind me.

Clark's machine disappeared over a hill. I neared the crest, anticipating the view. Instead, my snowmobile hurtled over an icy edge into a crevasse so suddenly that there wasn't even time to scream, let alone pray. I clutched the handlebars, bracing myself. For an instant I felt sickeningly weightless. Then the shock of impact ripped through my body and pain forked down my back.

I couldn't breathe. Snow gagged me. I tried to raise my arms to pull off my helmet, but I couldn't move. Then someone was pulling the helmet off me, sweeping snow from my face. I looked up to see Herb gasping for air. Behind him was Clark, clutching his injured arm. We'd all gone into the crevasse.

"Rich, say something," urged Herb, as his face twisted in pain.

"I can't move," I said.

"You're trapped under the machine. We'll try to get you out."

"Careful," I said, recalling the first-aid and EMT training I'd had years before. "I think my back is broken." I knew I shouldn't be moved too much. That meant hauling me out of the crevasse with ropes was out of the question. I would have to wait for a helicopter with a rescue basket and winch. If the cold didn't get me first.

Groaning from their own injuries, Clark and Herb managed to pull me from under the 600-pound snowmobile. Then I could clearly see how dire our situation was. I lay just a few feet from the edge of a sloping snow ledge that had apparently broken our fall. The ledge was about 15 feet wide, just big enough to support us and the twisted wreckage of our machines. I knew beyond its edge the crevasse plunged much deeper. I could hear water rushing along its bottom, far below. If the ledge gave way, they would never find our bodies.

A good 30 to 40 feet above us was the narrow oval opening to the chasm. We had never even seen it. Now it seemed so out of reach it may as well have been the sun. The rest of our group, one by one, peered into the abyss. They called down to us, but I was too dazed to make much sense of what they said.

"Someone's going back to Eureka to get help, Rich," Herb explained. "Just hold on." Our companions threw down water bottles and extra clothing. Hanging over us was a roof of ice. *What if that collapses?* I thought. *We'll be swept right over the edge.*

A spasm of pain shot through me. I heard my groan echo in the crevasse.

"Rich, are you okay?" asked Herb, bending over me.

The pain was so intense I couldn't even piece together a thought, much less speak it aloud.

"Rich," Herb called again.

"I'm cold," I managed to get out. He draped another jacket over me, but I couldn't stop shaking. It felt as if my insides were turning to ice. Finally, the men who had gone for help returned and threw down blankets. Herb and Clark covered me up to my chin.

"Helicopter's on its way," Herb told me. *What are they going to do when they get here?* I wondered, staring at the crevasse's narrow opening. The winds blew up to 100 mph over the ice fields. It would have to be perfectly still for a helicopter rescue. The odds were against it.

I turned my head away, trying to block those thoughts. The wall of the glacier before me, with countless blue-and-white striations marking its sleek face, was translucent. It seemed as though I could reach through it. Even there, even then, I was awestruck.

Herb and Clark kept talking to me, trying to keep me awake as waves of pain swept me in and out of consciousness. I lost track of time. All I knew was, I couldn't last much longer.

In a moment of clarity, I thought of Marge. She was probably worried sick, waiting for my call. Of course she would miss me, but with the children nearby she would be looked after. I'd had some rough times in my life—my divorce; caring for my deaf son, Jack, who has cerebral palsy—but overall, I felt blessed. I had looked forward to playing with our grandchildren, traveling, and snowmobiling with Marge for many more years, but I was grateful for the time I'd been given. *I'm not afraid,* I realized. Somehow, although death lay before me, I felt calm, certain, more serene than I'd ever felt while driving across the tundra. I had always gone to church, but never had I known a faith like this. *Jesus, I know I'm in Your hands,* I prayed. *Thank you for Your comfort. Please take care of my family and comfort them as You have me.*

"Tell Marge," I gasped to Herb through another spasm of pain, "how much I love her."

"You can tell her yourself, Rich. Listen!"

I heard a rumbling. Then a huge black shape loomed into view, blocking the sky. The chopper! It hovered directly above us in the remarkably still air. I watched as Clark and Herb were lifted to safety. The paramedics then had room to come down and ready me for rescue. One of them put his hand on my shoulder. "I've got you now," he said. I nearly broke down right there. I was going to live after all.

I was lifted out of the crevasse and rushed to the hospital. After five hours sprawled in the snow, my body temperature had plummeted to 84 degrees. Doctors immediately began warming me up to stabilize me for surgery. I had tubes running down my throat, so I couldn't speak. That night my family gathered around me. My son, Jack, signed to me. Clumsily, I signed back.

"He's responding. That's good," a doctor said to my wife. Still, I worried about my legs. I hadn't felt any of the test pokes and prods. Two days later, after 13 hours of back surgery, I still felt nothing below my waist. Then my doctor confirmed my fears. "I'm sorry," he told me, "but you'll never be able to walk again."

For a few weeks I kept telling my family I'd prove the doctor wrong. Facing the truth was hard, tougher than anything I'd faced before. With everyone rallying around me, I felt I had to stay upbeat for their sakes. But lying awake at night, watching Marge asleep in the chair by my bed, I gave in to depression. She had to help me get up, get dressed, go to the bathroom. *What a burden I am to her,* I thought. My condition made me angry and difficult sometimes. Yet Marge stayed by my side all day, every day.

One night I had a dream in which I was walking. It was so vivid and real that waking from it was like being told I was paralyzed all over again. I tried to muffle my sobs so I wouldn't wake Marge. *How do I go on, Lord?* I asked. *How can I live this way?*

Then the words of that paramedic came back to me. *I've got you now.* But it was God who was speaking. He'd had me in His hands when I plummeted into the crevasse and held on to me until I was rescued. I had put my trust in Him then, not afraid to die. Now I had to be not afraid to live.

After ten weeks in the hospital, I went home. A year later, I rode a snowmobile for the first time since the accident. It took a bit of extra work—I had to be secured to the machine and wear heavy clothing on my lower body—but it was well worth the effort. That first quick loop around a nearby lake was exhilarating. I put in 1,000 miles on my new machine last year, and I'm back at it this year. It has not been easy dealing with my limitations, but when I'm out there cruising over the tundra, Marge following in my tracks, I feel like myself again. God's canvas is as stunning as ever, and I am a part of it. The air is crisp, the ice glitters like diamonds, and when I look up at the incredibly blue sky, I think how good it is to be alive.

The Gift of Life

How beautiful it is to be alive!
To wake each morn as if the Maker's grace
Did us afresh from nothingness derive,
That we might sing "How happy is our case!
How beautiful it is to be alive."

HENRY SEPTIMUS SUTTON

The Music Box

BY SHIRLEY MILLER

My hobby is collecting music boxes—nothing expensive or rare or old, just music boxes I like and enjoy listening to. For years my mother's favorite was a figurine of an old woman sitting in a rocking chair and holding a few balloons.

Every time my mother came to visit me, she would go into the den and look at the music box and smile thoughtfully. Then she'd say, "If Dad goes first, that's me—sitting on a rocking chair in Lincoln Park, selling balloons." We would laugh. Then she would push the button and listen to the song it played: "Try to Remember" from the Fantasticks.

When Mother was nearly eighty, she suffered a mild stroke that put her in the hospital for a week. After that, she never became completely well again. Gradually her weakness increased. My father, who had been retired for several years, now became Mother's constant attendant. My sister and I took turns going over there one day a week to shop, clean house, and prepare casseroles and stews that my father could warm up for their meals.

Often my mother would ask me, "How's the old lady with the balloons?"

"Fine," I'd say. "She asks about you all the time." And we'd laugh.

Four years later my phone rang very early one morning. It was my father. He said, "Honey, you'd better get over here. It's Ma."

"What happened?" I asked, fearing the worst.

"She fell getting out of bed," he said. "I don't have the strength to lift her."

"I'll be right there," I said. I called my sister, told her the bad news, and said I'd pick her up on the way.

We found Mother sitting on the floor in her room, resting against her bed. Her face was sad and helpless, with tears of humiliation in her eyes. We got her back into bed.

"I'm sorry this happened," she whispered. "Thanks for coming. I'll make it up to you."

Those were her last words to us.

I called the doctor. An ambulance was there in minutes, but on the way to the hospital Mother lost consciousness. She was put into intensive care, while out in the waiting room the doctor told us, "It's very bad. There's been a lot of brain damage. She may not come out of this."

It was the beginning of a long ordeal for all of us. Mother went into a coma. Ten days later she was transferred to a private room where we could stay with her all day.

I was there every day, all day. Mother remained in a coma, but I talked to her anyway, hoping she could somehow hear me.

"We're all praying for you, Ma," I told her, "everybody—even the old lady with the balloons."

Early in the morning on November 19, with our house still in darkness, the phone rang. I braced myself. "Hello?"

"Mrs. Miller, this is the head nurse at the hospital. I'm sorry to have to tell you that your mother died ten minutes ago."

Even though I had been expecting them, her words were like a blow. "Thank you," I managed to say somehow. "I'll take care of everything." As I hung up, I glanced at the clock. It was 5:10 a.m. My mother had died at five a.m., after being in a coma for forty-nine days.

Somehow we all got through the next few days. Then came the strain of adjusting to the loss, of waiting for the sorrow to fade. Time passed, but the sorrow did not disappear. When death takes a loved one, even though you trust in the promise of everlasting life, something in you longs for reassurance, for proof of that promise. It's only human, I guess.

The months went by. One season slipped into another. One day, my husband Lenny came home from work with a bad cold. I suggested that he spend a couple of days in bed, but he said he had too much work to do at the office and couldn't spare the time. A few days later, the cold was so bad that he had no choice. I nursed him all day, and then, so he could sleep undisturbed, I spent the night on the sofa in the den.

It had been a hard day for me, because it was the day before the first anniversary of Mother's death. I kept thinking about her, missing her, wishing she were only a telephone call away. It would have been so helpful just to talk to her, to ask her advice about Lenny, to feel the warmth and reassurance she always gave.

Tired and worried about Lenny, I tossed fitfully on the sofa for a while. I kept thinking about all the uncertainties of life, and I felt lost and lonely, somehow. I missed our familiar bed and Lenny's comforting presence. Finally I drifted off into a restless sleep.

Hours later I woke with a start; something strange, something unfamiliar had wakened me. For a moment I didn't know what it was. Then I heard the music. The soft sounds of a familiar song drifted through my mind. But where was it coming from? There was darkness all around me. Had I been dreaming it? No, the music was still playing. In the darkness I could hear its eerie tinkling.

I sat up. I stared into the gloom. There, on the desk, was the silhouette of the old lady with the balloons, and the song I heard coming from the music box was my mother's favorite, "Try to Remember."

"But it can't be playing," I said to myself. "Nobody's touched it. And the last time I played that box I distinctly remember letting it run down!"

And then I remembered what day it was. November 19. I glanced at the desk clock. It was five a.m. Ma had died exactly one year ago to the day, to the hour, to the minute! I began to cry. I whispered to the dark: "If that's you, Ma, I hope you're safe and happy. You know that we still love you and miss you and, yes, we still remember."

I lay down again, weeping, listening to the music until it stopped, and I fell asleep, reassured at last.

I awoke again around seven thirty and smelled bacon. I got up and went to the kitchen. There was Lenny, shaved, fully dressed, at the stove frying bacon and eggs. "You were so sound asleep that I decided to fix breakfast myself," he said. "I'm going to work."

I stared at him, astonished. "Are you well enough for that?"

"Yes," he said. "During the night, the cold just seemed to melt out of me. I feel great."

I felt as if I were going to cry again. "I'll do that," I said. I took the spatula away from Lenny and turned my back to him, close to tears.

Lenny went to the table and sat down to his cup of coffee. He said, "Tell me something. Did I hear you playing Ma's music box during the night, or did I dream it?"

I fought the tears. I couldn't talk about it yet.

"No," I said. "I didn't play it."

And in my heart I thanked the Lord for using a little mechanical music box to let us know that our mother was safe with Him, that she still loved us, still missed us, and, yes, still remembered.

The Music of Love

From the heart of God comes the strongest rhythm—the rhythm of love.... And so the work of the human heart, it seems to me, is to listen for that music and pick up on its rhythms.

KEN GIRE

Please Show Me the Way

BY STEVE KENNEDY

On a warm, late-summer day, a baby boy was born. Not a bright-eyed, rosy-checked, cooing, perfect baby, but a tiny, frail, fretful, imperfect baby. His chest labored as he fought for every breath, his body blue and cold. His legs were twisted like gnarled tree roots, a pitiful sight to see. The doctor just shook his head and hid the child from the anxious, exhausted mother so she would not be alarmed...for surely the child would not live. The nurses scurried out of the delivery room with the tot wrapped in soft, warm blankets and placed him in a very special room with lights and machines that hummed and pumped and had wires and tubes. The doctors crowded around the child—all these minds, trained to heal, together for one tiny life. The decisions were made, but the prognosis was the same: the child would not live.

The young parents were told, and weeping overcame the mother like a racking, tearing pain, while the father sat in stony silence, afraid to move for fear reality might overtake him.

A sympathetic nurse called the hospital chaplain so the young parents would not have to shoulder this unbearable thing alone. The chaplain came immediately, an understanding, serene, and gentle man, a gladiator against sorrow. The parents told him of their son and their fears. What would they feel when they saw the grotesque form of life that lay in the special room? This was their new baby boy, the child they had so wanted and had loved even before birth. The man of mercy understood their fears, for he had seen many sorrows, and calmed the distraught parents with his kind and reassuring words and faith.

After many hours the three were told that they could see the child. The parents drew upon that strength that is hidden somewhere, waiting to be drawn upon, like a deep, cool well. The child lay amidst machines with blinking lights, video screens, and sucking sounds. White, red, and yellow bottles, swinging like small kites, extended over his head. He was so tiny that he looked lost in the glass box, his new bed.

The parents' shocked look began to fade, and a small smile played at the corners of the mother's mouth. Why, he had his father's hair, like golden wheat, and pale blue eyes, the color of the lake at home. His fingers were long, and his nose was his grandfather's for sure. True, his color was bluish and his legs were a twisted mass of flesh and bones. But the Lord is kind; and through loving eyes, the parents did not see that ugliness— only a beautiful child, struggling with every labored breath to stay alive.

The chaplain said a prayer, a short, fervent prayer for life. This was the child's first introduction to Christ, but during the long days and nights that followed, the child would hear the prayers of many. After a few weeks, the doctors' frowns began to relax, and with caution they told the parents there was now a chance, a hope, that they might have been wrong and the child might live. It would not be an easy life, for there were many problems other than those so easily visible. But there was a chance, a miraculous chance.

As the days and then years passed, each problem presented itself and each crisis was met, each in its own way and time. The child learned the comfort, strength, and peace of prayer and in accepting God's will. There were prayers as surgery approached and his legs began to form. Prayers for the relief of itching from body casts that seemed to be a permanent part of his young life. Prayers for medication to be found to control his frightening convulsions, and prayers of thanks when it was indeed discovered. Prayers for the men and women who guided his body through years of physical therapy. Most of all were the prayers for patience and understanding when things did not go as fast as the boy had hoped or the way he had hoped they would.

The doctors were right; life has not always been easy for this child. He has stood under the teasing and taunting of unthinking peers and the limitations that his body makes upon him, not without tears and frustration. But all things are possible with God's help.

You see, I am the boy in this story, and I know what God's grace and mercy can do. I have heard the story of my birth many times, and I believe that God saved my life for some reason known only to Him. I can only try to live my life the way He directs, and I'm sure He will show me the way. He has done all right so far.

God Is My Strength

My flesh and my heart may fail, but God is the strength of my heart and my portion forever.

PSALM 73:26 NIV

Ripley's Believe It or Not

BY SHAUNA KATTLER

The day finally came that we had long been dreading. My husband Dean and I knew it was time to say good-bye to our beloved golden retriever, Ripley. The vet was coming over that afternoon. That morning we took him to the park, knowing it was going to be the last time he would ever play ball.

For thirteen years, not a day went by that we didn't play ball. Now I bounced the ball on the pavement in front of the cart Ripley sat on, and he weakly tried to catch it in his mouth. The past couple of weeks his breathing had worsened and he gasped for air.

Dean touched my shoulder. "Just a little bit longer," I said. I knew putting Ripley down was the best choice, but I wasn't ready. Not yet.

How could I let him go? He'd been with Dean and me almost as long as we'd been married. We didn't have children, so our dogs became our kids. We moved often for Dean's work—we'd lived in Castlegar, Kelown, and Vancouver in British Columbia and then in Seattle before moving to San Jose, California. The dogs were my anchor and helped me feel settled no matter where we lived.

My parents gave us Ripley as a Christmas present when he was just ten weeks old, a month after Dean and I got married. His thick, downy, blond fur, black-button nose, and chubby stature made him look like a baby polar bear. His huge paws were an indication of the one-hundred-pound adult he would become. As with all new parents, we showered Ripley with attention. Dean even invented a game. He'd lie down on the floor next to our puppy and toss a tennis ball into the air, and Ripley would use Dean's stomach as a springboard, launching into the air, and catch the ball before it could hit the ground.

I had my own game with Ripley. I sat at the bottom of the stairs while he sat at the top holding a ball in his mouth. He'd let the ball drop and watch, fascinated, as the ball bounced down the steps one at a time. When it hit the last step, I caught it and tossed it back to him. Each time he caught the ball, he gnawed it like it was the first one he had ever seen. He never tired of this game and could play it for hours.

The following Christmas Dean brought home Holly, a small female golden. The two dogs quickly became inseparable. It wasn't until shortly after his tenth birthday that we discovered Ripley's true nose for the ball. Specifically baseballs. Dean and I had just moved from one neighborhood in Seattle to another. Nearby was a large park where we walked every day, with mulched paths, shady trees, and plenty of squirrels that Holly loved to chase. Ripley, however, had other things on his mind besides squirrels. One day his nose caught a scent and he veered into the bushes. "What did you find, Ripley?" I asked. His tail was going round and round like a windmill, so I could tell it had to be something really good. He emerged triumphant with a baseball in his mouth. "Good boy!" I said, kneeling down to give him a hug.

That was just the beginning. There were seven baseball fields at the park, and every time we went there, Ripley was on a mission. He'd zigzag in and out of the bushes or under the bleachers and come trotting back with a baseball in his mouth. Sometimes he'd stop in front of a bush, his tail wagging, look at me, then stare pointedly back at the bush. That meant he'd located a baseball he couldn't extract. Even if I couldn't see it right away, he'd stand there unwavering, as if to say, "I know it's there." Sure enough, after digging around on my hands and knees, I'd find a ball tangled in the underbrush.

As Ripley's collection of baseballs grew, we resorted to collecting them in a trash can in the garage. On average, he found one or two a day. His record in one day was twelve! I felt like a mom who'd just seen her kid hit a home run.

Ripley found 220 baseballs that year. We donated them to the Little League. A few newspapers picked up the story and Ripley became a minor celebrity. No one could quite explain where all the balls came from. Had the Little Leaguers really lost that many?

The next year Ripley found 330 baseballs! When the off-season came, however, he seemed sluggish on our walks. I noticed he was dragging one of his hind legs.

The paralysis got worse. Numerous trips to the vet couldn't diagnose the problem and an MRI came back inconclusive. I bought a back-end harness to hoist up Ripley's rear as I walked him. Soon it was Little League season again, and even with his disability, Ripley found 150 baseballs. However, I couldn't keep half-carrying him everywhere we went. I outweighed Ripley by only twelve pounds, and my whole body ached from supporting his weight. "Come on, Ripley," I snapped one time. "You can walk faster!" Yet when I looked into his eyes, they told me he was doing the best he could. *God*, I prayed, *there's got to be a better way. Please help Ripley. Help me.*

I was out shopping for plants one day and spied a large flat garden cart. That was it! Perfect for hauling Ripley. I immediately bought one. From the moment we lifted Ripley onto it, he was as happy as a dog let loose in a room full of bacon (or in his case, baseballs). Ripley loved riding in his cart to the park.

When Ripley was twelve years old, Dean got transferred again, to California. Two weeks before we were due to move to San Jose, I felt two lumps on both sides of Ripley's neck. I took him to the vet, and this time there was a diagnosis: lymphoma. The word chilled me. Ripley started chemotherapy.

I took the dogs for walks at the park in San Jose three times a day. Though the park didn't have any baseball diamonds, I knew Ripley loved being there. We developed a new game where I bounced the tennis ball in front of Ripley's cart and he'd catch it in his mouth and gnaw on it. I'd walk over and grab the slimy ball from him and toss it back again. I got more exercise than Ripley, but he loved it and that was all that mattered.

Due to Ripley's condition, we got a lot of attention at the park. "I see you here with your dogs every day and admire your commitment," one woman said, even offering to help if I ever needed a break. Another woman brought me coffee and a bag of donuts, saying, "It warms my heart, how you care for him." A firefighter stopped me to tell me how much he appreciated my dedication to my dog.

One summer day a group of women came up to us. "Can we pray with you?" one of them said. In the middle of the park, these strangers encircled Ripley and me, and together we prayed. I needed it. The chemo wasn't working and Ripley was getting worse.

Now the lymph nodes on either side of his throat were so swollen it was hard for him to breathe. I tried to comfort him as much as I could. Finally, Dean urged me to make the call to the vet. We had this one last morning in the park with Ripley.

I bounced his ball to him for a few more minutes and Ripley played as best he could. Finally, we took him home.

The vet arrived. Dean and I wrapped our arms around Ripley one last time, sobbing as we said our good-byes. Then our golden boy was gone.

I don't know how long I'd been crying when Dean suggested we take Holly for a walk. "It'll be good for us to get out of the house," he said. Reluctantly, I agreed.

We pulled Ripley's cart out, the same one he'd sat on just hours earlier. Holly climbed aboard. She glanced from side to side. "Where's Ripley?" her eyes seemed to ask. Dean and I headed down the street in silence.

We'd just walked into the park when something lying in the grass caught my eye. Something white.

A baseball.

I looked around. There were no ball fields here. There wasn't even anyone near us. No kids playing catch, no dogs playing fetch. Just Holly, Dean, and me.

I picked up the baseball and held it to my heart. I didn't have to wonder where this ball came from. I knew.

A Touch of Wonder

There is not enough darkness in all the world to put out the light of one small candle.... There are always certain things to cling to. Little things usually...any reminder of something deeply felt or dearly loved. No one is so poor as not to have many of these small candles. When they are lighted, darkness goes away and a touch of wonder remains.

ARTHUR GORDON

The Phone Call I Never Made

BY MONA SCHREIBER

One day several years ago, my next-door neighbor phoned me while I was busily scraping some dried cereal off a bowl. "Have you read the paper today?" she asked.

"No," I answered, mildly curious. I reached for the paper.

"It's Pastor Reinboth. He's dead."

At that moment my eyes fell on his picture in the paper. "Oh, no, it can't be," I gasped. And the persistent thought flooded my mind, *It's too late. You're too late.*

We must have continued talking, but I scarcely remember what we said. I hung up the phone and pushed the paper aside. Outside my window the rain was heavy, as heavy as my grief.

Can it really be a year since I met him? I thought.

That particular day a year before, the carpet installers were to come and the living room was a confusion of piled-up furniture. I was hoping the day would soon be over when the doorbell rang. I opened the door. There stood a minister, wearing a turned-around collar.

He smiled broadly. "I'm Pastor Reinboth, the new pastor at the Lutheran church we're building here." I waited to hear a request for a donation. It never came.

"I've been going from door to door to meet the people in town," he explained.

I wasn't sure what I should do next. I smiled. There was an uncomfortable silence. His graying hair made me think that he might be tired after all that walking around.

"Look," I said, "I'm Jewish. I don't know anything about Lutheran ministers, but if you'd like to come in and rest a bit, you're welcome."

To my surprise he accepted. I fumbled around the piled-up furniture and pulled out two chairs. He perched on his and we chatted. At first words came slowly. We talked about the Midwest, where he had come from, about his wife and family who were to join him soon. Then he leaned forward eagerly. "Perhaps I'm foolish, walking around like this, introducing myself to everyone. But a minister should not be a remote individual seen only in a pulpit. He should talk to people, know them, help them."

I liked his eagerness, his smile. "That's the concept we have of a rabbi," I said. " 'Rabbi' really means 'teacher,' and a teacher should be among people."

He looked up at the portrait of a rabbi above our mantel. My husband had painted it. It had a dark, brooding feeling; suffering was in the eyes.

"Who did that?" Pastor Reinboth asked. "It's awfully good. Those suffering eyes. I'm reminded of Christ on the cross."

I stared at the familiar picture, startled that "my" rabbi was similar to Christ. But I saw what he meant. Christ was a rabbi too, and there is a universality about suffering. I mentioned that.

"Yes," he said. "That's true. The important thing, when we see suffering, is to share and help with it."

I offered him a cup of coffee. There wasn't a thing to go with it except some graham crackers. But he was delighted. "Umm, good," he said and popped a cracker into his mouth.

He was interested in everything—a story I was writing, the problems of ghetto children, the new life he would find here in California. We talked on and on. It was as if a sister had found a brother, though they hadn't known each other existed.

When my husband came home an hour or so later, he was a bit startled to find the pastor there, but he liked him as much as I did. By the time Mr. Reinboth left, we all agreed to get together with him and his wife when she arrived in a few weeks.

There was much to do in the next few weeks. The baby got the croup. When she got well, I started a college course. I thought of Mr. Reinboth often and was going to have his wife over. I even began to plan a party. But suddenly Christmas was here. I wanted to call them. I really did. But almost a year had passed and it would be embarrassing to call after all that time. I felt a bit foolish. Still, I meant to have a party for them....

Now he was dead. He was fifty-six, younger than I thought. He took sick while in the pulpit and apologized for having to leave, then collapsed of a heart attack.

I grieved, and was surprised that I did. I grieved not only for my loss but for all the people in his church. Then I thought, *His poor family has suffered the greatest loss. What of his wife?* My first inclination was to call her. Impulsively I reached for the phone then stopped. What on earth could I say to a woman I had never met? What solace could I offer? I didn't even know her husband's first name.

Then a quiet voice seemed to speak inside me: *"You made one mistake by never calling him. Are you going to do the same thing all over again with his wife? He loved her. She must be wonderful if he loved her. Sharing a sorrow is still sharing. That's what he said."*

I called her. We are like sisters now. His first name was Sam.

Seize the Opportunity

Today is unique! It has never occurred before and it will never be repeated. At midnight it will end, quietly, suddenly, totally. Forever. But the hours between now and then are opportunities with eternal possibilities.

CHARLES R. SWINDOLL

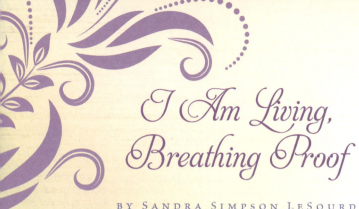

I Am Living, Breathing Proof

BY SANDRA SIMPSON LESOURD

I n the living room of a cozy ranch house nestled next to the rim-rock cliffs that border Billings, Montana, a group of women sat with clasped hands and bowed heads. "Dear Lord," Marlene said, "we're here to pray for Sandy. She's in deep trouble. She doesn't know we are praying for her, but Lord, we ask humbly that You be with her and strengthen her."

At that same moment, I sat in Warm Springs, Montana, staring through the grime-streaked windows of the State Hospital for Mental Disorders. My weight was over 200 pounds, my skin was gray, and my hair was greasy—a sad situation for someone who had represented her home state of Vermont at the Miss America Pageant in Atlantic City.

How had I got myself into such a miserable condition? There's a lot of scientific jargon to describe compulsive personalities like mine. My motto since my teen years had been: Anything worth doing is worth overdoing. I would tell people, "When my motor is running, I can't seem to shut it off."

And eventually my compulsive overdoing resulted in debilitating addictions to everything from alcohol, prescription drugs, and nicotine to overeating and out-of-control shopping sprees.

"It's time to start," said Marlene. They were meeting again as they did every Thursday morning, these ten or twelve women from the First United Methodist Church in Billings. After opening with songs of praise, there were prayers of thanksgiving—and then progress reports about the people they'd been praying for. The meetings generally lasted about two hours, each woman bringing a notebook to record the prayers they'd be making throughout the week. Special prayer attention was focused on the group's "Ten-Most-Wanted List," a list they had compiled, containing desperate cases of people most in need of the Lord: a teenager on drugs, a mother with Alzheimer's, a husband in the last stages of cancer, and a recent "most wanted" addition—Sandy.

So many people had tried unsuccessfully to help me: my family, friends, counselors and psychiatrists, including those at a treatment center where I'd spent a month. I put my head in my hands. It seemed hopeless. Could I ever go home? Would I ever be whole again?

Since the group believed in the power released by affirming the best in the person being prayed for, over and over they inserted Sandy's name into Scripture verses: "Strength and dignity are [Sandy's] clothing.... [Sandy] opens her mouth with wisdom, and the teaching of kindness is on her tongue...her children rise up and call her blessed" (Proverbs 31:25–26, 28).

And then the women asked God "to transform Sandy, send Your emissaries across her path to witness to her, to free her from bondage."

I was in bondage—to a suicidal depression and spiritual darkness. Every time I closed my eyes, an inky black curtain fell across my conscious mind, and I was unable to summon any positive or pleasing visual images. It was terrifying to be lying in bed with my eyes closed and see nothing but forbidding night— or worse, evil, mocking faces.

One day a young woman named Karen entered the hospital and was assigned to a room adjacent to mine. Her fiancé, it was reported, had been killed in an accident. Karen was inconsolable. Over and over she kept crying out, "Help me, Jesus! Help me, Jesus!"

Karen's constant yelling was aggravating. And the worst thing was, she attached herself to me. I tried to avoid Karen, but she followed me, her dark brown eyes pleading for me to help her.

Then, on a sultry July night, I was tossing restlessly in my hospital bed when I sensed a presence. I sat up. Karen was standing in the doorway, her white robe startlingly bright in the moonlight.

She approached my bed, crying softly. "Oh, Sandy, does Jesus love me? Does Jesus really love me?" I could tell from her pleading voice that this was the only thing in the world that mattered to her.

What to do? What to say? I longed to comfort this weeping young woman but felt incapable of reassuring anybody of anything. Yet I had to do something. Taking Karen in my arms, I stroked her damp hair. It had been a long time since I'd held anyone or offered comfort—I'd always been the one demanding it.

I cleared my throat awkwardly. "Yes, Karen," I said. "Jesus—"

I stopped in astonishment. My heart was beating furiously, and I felt warm and cold at the same time. What was I saying to this young woman? Why were these words having such power over her—and over me? "Karen," I said, "Jesus loves you. He really does."

Her sobbing stopped in an instant. She wiped her eyes with the back of her hand, thanked me in a voice of childlike gratitude, and slipped out of my room and back to hers.

I lay back down, puzzled at the strange lightness, almost giddiness, that I was feeling. The room seemed filled with a fragrant coolness.

"[Sandy] opens her mouth with wisdom, and the teaching of kindness is on her tongue...her children rise up and call her blessed."

Thursday morning. The intercessors were meeting. "Dear Lord," Naomi said, leading the others in prayer, "God did not give [Sandy] a spirit of timidity but a spirit of power and love and self-control" (2 Timothy 1:7). "And with His stripes [Sandy is] healed" (Isaiah 53:5).

A few days after Karen's nighttime visit to my room, she left the hospital just as suddenly as she had arrived. I puzzled about what had happened between us; for the first time in my long illness—and almost against my will—I seemed to have helped another person.

Was there something different happening to me? A glimmer of joy here, a flicker of wonder there? I'd been noticing the birds outside my window, a rose in a vase in the patients' lounge, the picture of a child in the recreation area.

I stared out the window into a small grassy courtyard. The morning sun had appeared over the building annex, casting shadows from a slatted roof overhang into my room. Across my skirt and onto the floor fell a pattern of stripes. Out of nowhere, words came into my mind: *And with His stripes we are healed.*

They sounded scriptural, but what did I know about the Bible? Could I have heard those words as a child in Sunday school? Strange, yet the words were strongly, deeply reassuring. Was it possible that I could get better after all?

Marge, Loretta, Eva, Dottie, Betty, Bess—the prayer witnesses were faithful to their tasks. Many of them prayed not only on Thursdays but on every day of the week too, sometimes aloud during morning and evening devotions, sometimes silently while waiting in line at checkout counters or sitting in traffic. Again and again their prayers went out: "[Sandy] can do all things in Him who strengthens [her]" (Philippians 4:13).

To everyone's surprise, including my own, I was making such good progress, that for the first time, the hospital staff felt I might make it on my own. A visit home was in order.

The first morning back in Billings in my own bed, I awoke terrified. How could I make it up to my family for all my irresponsible behavior over the past fifteen years? Feelings of guilt and fear overwhelmed me. *Sleep in,* came the tempting voice inside my head. *Stay right here in bed.* That was the way I had handled things in the past.

But a new voice inside me spoke. *Get up and get going. Now!*

The old ways were entrenched, though, resistant to something new. I was afraid. No, I'd stay in bed today and start my new life tomorrow.

Get up. Do it now! The voice wouldn't stop—and I actually started to think I might enjoy getting on with my life. I got up, showered, put in a load of wash, made an appointment to have my hair cut, and mopped the kitchen floor.

Major victories! As I moved from task to task, I was aided by a new inner feeling, a positive inner reinforcement that could be gentle and encouraging but at the same time insistent and strong. In the past my inner voice had always been negative, undermining and relentlessly critical. Now I felt a resolve and new sense of purpose that shocked me.

Another Thursday. For over a year the group in Billings had been praying for the woman with the severe problems of addiction. Once again they bowed their heads and said, "We know that in everything God works for good with [Sandy] who [loves] Him" (Romans 8:28).

But at this meeting there was a difference: I was sitting among them.

On a bright June morning I walked into a living room filled with smiling women who welcomed me warmly. My neighbor Kathy had invited me, and I perched nervously on the edge of a green sofa, waiting to see what all this "intercessory prayer" was about. I learned for the first time about the prayers that had gone up for me during my darkest days. I still needed much healing, but I was on my way.

Week after week I joined them in their prayers for others and for myself. Then, when I left Billings once again for a treatment center and halfway house, they continued their prayers. And later when I moved to Vermont to start a new life, I continued to call or write them. Their prayers were making a difference in my life, and I knew it.

I was almost destroyed by my extreme compulsive-addictive behavior. I know that most of us suffer from one kind of addiction or another, many from cross-addiction. Professional counseling is important, but I'm convinced that steady, all-out, unremitting prayer is crucial in a person's recovery. God uses intercessory prayer to heal, to restore, and to redeem the lost. For person after person struggling with problems that seem insurmountable, this sort of intercessory prayer has produced miraculous results.

Today I am living, breathing proof that prayers for others—intercessory prayers—are one of the most powerful tools that God has placed in our hands. My recovery did not take place in a month or even a year. It was a long process. Even nowadays, every so often, the tendency toward addictive behavior beckons me back to the old habits. It's then that I say my own prayer: "I, Sandy, can do all things through Christ who strengthens me." Then I bow my head, insert somebody else's name—and pass the prayer along for another.

The Power of Prayer

If we truly love people, we will desire for them far more than that which is within our power to give them, and this will lead us to prayer. Intercession is a way of loving others.

RICHARD J. FOSTER

The Night I Grew Up

BY JOHN MCLAUGHLIN

I think I grew up one night in a hospital parking lot, underneath my desperately ill father's window.

When you're a kid, your life covers such a small area—places, people, events, thoughts, and dreams all revolve about you. Even at seventeen, I guess I was pretty self-centered. Unhappiness was only something read about in newspapers. The only problems I faced were those any young person can expect: what career to follow, school grades that could be higher, and raising money for all the extra things that make a teenager's life more interesting.

Death was something I thought about from time to time but not with any real concern. After all, Mother, Dad, my sister Nancy, who was twelve, and I were all pretty healthy, and even if my grandparents were getting on in years, they, too, were well. At seventeen you don't think too much of death.

I gave little thought to the important things in life, and I especially veered away from anything remotely religious or spiritual.

When I was much younger, I went to church because I was encouraged to do so by my parents. I always disliked it and resented having to go.

"It's just a waste of time," I'd complain. Finally I stopped attending. I didn't need Sunday school or God, I thought.

Then one summer I found out how wrong I was.

I loved my father as any boy loves a good father. However, I seldom let him know this. We were close —Dad and I—but it wasn't a closeness of speech as much as a quiet sharing.

I remember those golden times when just the two of us would pack and go off camping for a few days. Or those happy ventures to the river to do a little fishing. These were times of quiet joy and I would trade them for nothing.

There was a way Dad had that added an extra special light to whatever he said, whether it was telling a joke or commenting on something of a more serious nature.

He never preached, yet I remember some of the things he told me, not in vague recall, but in crystal clearness that hits my mind with no less pronouncement than the sound of the loudest church bell on Sunday. One thing especially stands out.

One year, during summer vacation, I told him I did no thinking about God.

"I'm not sure I even believe there is a God," I said.

I expected Dad to be shocked, I guess, or at least to argue with me because he had his own deep faith. But not Dad.

"Don't worry about it. It's not unusual for a young man, growing up, to start questioning. God will understand your searching for truth." He told me to repeat the words, "Lord, help Thou mine unbelief" (from Mark 9:24).

"Someday your mind will surely change," Dad reassured me.

He was right, for I changed it in the course of the very next week.

The day following our conversation I came home from my summer job for lunch. Dad was washing Mother's car. He always was doing something to help Mother. I waved to him, went into the house, ate, and then rushed off to work. Dad was still washing the car, in T-shirt and old pants, his balding head gleaming in the sun. He said a few everyday words to me, and I said a few to him. There was nothing special about it, but I'll always remember that scene.

That afternoon he had a stroke. Nancy told me about it when I came home from work.

"There's nothing to worry about," she said. We weren't to go to the hospital. Mother was with Dad and we were to see him when he felt a little better.

The next day, thinking Dad was safe and recovering, I went on enjoying my carefree life.

That evening when I came home Mother told me the sad news: Dad had had a second major stroke. There was absolutely no chance for recovery.

I did not cry. I showed no emotion. I could not even comfort my mother. I was numb. I couldn't think of anything but Dad: Dad was dying and I'd never see him again.

I was truly in a state of shock. Shock is a great shelter for a grieving person. It keeps you from really thinking. I went to bed that night hoping that Mother and the doctors were wrong, that Dad would live.

But the days ahead held out no hope. Dad was sinking. One night, I could not stay home. Something compelled me to try to get closer to Dad. I drove out to the hospital parking lot and got out of the car. I looked up at the windows, trying to figure out which one was Dad's. When I had located it, I stood staring. I think this was the first time that I really knew I would not see him again.

And standing there, release came. Tears rolled down my cheeks. Out loud, in a shaky voice, I said, "Good-bye, Dad," and at that moment, I felt something come over me that I cannot explain.

It seemed suddenly that Dad had replied to me. I was beneath the window. My voice had been low. He could not have heard me. Indeed, even if he had, he would have been too deep in semiconsciousness to respond. He replied, not in a way that can be heard nor even known for sure, yet I knew he had said:

"Do not grieve, son. You can't realize how soon we will meet again."

I got back in the car and drove home. And with me went the certainty that death, when it came, would not be the end—that what Dad had said was true.

He died the next morning.

The week between Dad's stroke and his funeral was surely the unhappiest in my life, and yet it did something to change me. I guess you can say I grew up overnight.

This was my first experience with the sadness of life, and I saw in a moment that life must have its pain as well as its joy, that this is not yet the perfect world.

I discovered that Dad was many things to many people. He had been a wonderful father to Nancy and me. He had been a beloved husband to my mother. He was greatly respected by his company for being an efficient, pleasant, and conscientious insurance adjuster. He had written stories as a hobby, and several had been used on Voice of America. I am proud of all my father was to others and to me.

And suddenly there were other people in my world—not the way they'd always been there—in relation to me. Now they were there as individuals and I had to find my place in relation to them. I couldn't provide the help and companionship that Dad had given Mother, but I could—in my new grown-up status— give some comfort. And I could guide my sister in a way that might take the place of my father to some extent. I was conscious, too, of a new resolve to do something constructive with my life.

Suddenly God was in my world too. When sadness overwhelmed me and I found it impossible to cope with, I turned the whole thing over to God. I could actually feel His presence, sustaining and strengthening me. It was so real that I no longer doubted His existence. It was just as Dad had predicted— "Someday your mind will surely change."

Of course, there is still grief for all of us. There is missing Dad and regretting the lost opportunities to know him better and to tell him of our love. But now I feel the gentle hand of God reaching out to take mine, and I can, with deep belief, turn to Him for comfort. It gives a wonderful sense of peace.

Strength and Peace

Character cannot be developed in ease and quiet.
Only through experience of trial and suffering
can the soul be strengthened, ambition
inspired, and success achieved.

HELEN KELLER

Woman Alone

BY KATHRYN KELLER

A flash of red by our snow-covered barn caused me to catch my breath. For a moment I thought it was my husband, wearing his favorite flannel shirt. But it wasn't my husband. It was only a bird. Silently, I hated the creature for the memory it had provoked. Tears filled my eyes, and the bird—though offended by my gaze—flew away.

It was winter, and my husband was dead. Three months before, he had suffered a heart attack while working around the buildings of our small dairy farm. He had been 42 years old.

How long, I thought, *will I continue to suffer this sense of loss? When will I ever be whole again?* My husband's death had torn in my heart a gaping hole that refused to heal.

Numbly, I turned from the window and walked to the kitchen. While setting a place for lunch, I stared blankly at the single seam that cut across the center of the table. Yesterday there had been two seams, but this morning I had removed the table's leaf and stored it in the cellar. With my husband gone, there was no need for the extra setting. *How nice it would be,* I thought bitterly, *to be able to adjust to change as easily as this table—to just snap together and carry on as usual.* Again I felt the hot sting of tears. Never had I felt so alone.

My entire life had always revolved around my family, and now, it seemed, there was none. John, our 22-year-old son, had recently received a promotion and been transferred halfway across the country to Colorado. Shelley, our 18-year-old daughter, was away at school in Minneapolis.

"But, Mom,"—John had approached me after the funeral—"I don't have to stay in Colorado. I don't like the idea of you being all alone. Considering the circumstances, I'm sure my boss will let me return to my old job."

"No," I had replied firmly. "This promotion is too important to your career for you to pass it by. Please don't worry about me. I'll be fine."

About the same time, Shelley caught me alone in the family room.

"Really, Mother," she said, "I don't have to go back to college. Or I could transfer to a school closer to home."

"No, you won't," I said. "You've had your heart set on college since you were a little girl. You're settled there now and doing well. I think you should stay."

Deep down inside I would have given anything if either one of the children could have stayed. But I knew they had their own lives to lead. It was important to let them go.

In the days following my husband's funeral, there had been much to do. After saying good-bye to the children, I sold our cattle and rented out the land. But once the flurry of post-funeral activities ended, with each passing day I grew more and more depressed.

I just couldn't get used to being a widow. I tried reading books on the subject, but they only seemed to heighten my sense of aloneness. When lunchtime came, I still half-expected to hear the creak of the back door opening, the sound of my husband stamping his muddy work boots on the mat. Gradually, my depression became so bad that I often chose not to answer the phone, and—except to buy groceries—I rarely left the house. Sometimes I watched television, but I never seemed to remember a thing I'd seen or heard. Not even my favorite pastimes—oil painting, needlepoint, long walks—appealed to me. I had neither energy nor interest.

When I wasn't depressed, I was angry. Anything that reminded me of my husband aroused my fury: our favorite song on the radio, a glimpse of the fir tree we had planted together, even the calls and visits of well-meaning friends.

Most of all, I was angry at God. From the day of the funeral, I stopped going to church. I dropped out of women's groups. If God was indeed a personal God, then He was cruel and heartless. Otherwise, how could He have allowed my husband to die?

At the sound of the doorbell, I frowned with annoyance. Why couldn't people leave me alone? Quietly, I got up and peered through the peephole in the door. It was my neighbor Marcella. While other friends had stopped calling, Marcella was persistent. Not a week passed without her stopping by.

I opened the door.

"Kaye!" she exclaimed, with her cheery smile. "Mind if I come in?"

"All right," I said dully. "I'm just fixing lunch."

I made grilled cheese sandwiches, and we sat at the kitchen table. After chatting for about ten minutes, Marcella became suddenly serious.

"Kaye," she said. "I'm worried about you. You've got to stop brooding. This can't go on forever, you know."

"I know," I said.

"Did you ever consider seeing a doctor?" she asked. "You're under a lot of stress. Maybe he can give you something to help."

I said nothing.

"Well, that does it," said Marcella, reaching for the kitchen phone. "I'm making an appointment for you right now. What's your doctor's number?"

For some reason, I didn't resist. I gave Marcella the number and she made an appointment for the following morning.

The doctor prescribed tranquilizers, little blue pills. I was depressed, he explained, a natural reaction to the death of a loved one. The pills would help.

Used as prescribed, the pills did have a calming effect. They did nothing, however, to ease my heartache or loneliness. One day, just to see what would happen, I increased the dosage. It worked. That is, like a sort of emotional novocaine, it helped me to forget. As weeks passed by, I found myself having to increase the dosage still more to achieve the desired effect. My morning coffee was preceded by one pill, my afternoon tea by two, and another was needed at bedtime in order for me to sleep through the night. Occasionally I worried about the number of pills I was taking, but I talked myself out of any real fears. The pills made me feel better, I told myself. The doctor had prescribed them. Besides, I could stop taking them any time I wanted to.

Still, with five pharmacies in town, I staggered my visits to each so that no one would suspect my habit. All that was needed to renew the prescription was the label from the previous bottle.

The only time I didn't use the pills was when I was with my children. It wasn't that I didn't want them to know; rather, their company filled my loneliness to the extent that I didn't need the pills. When December arrived, the first anniversary of my husband's death, Shelley was able to spend her entire three-week Christmas vacation at home. It was wonderful. We shopped, laughed, had long talks and stayed up late watching television and eating popcorn. I never took a pill, But the morning of Shelley's departure, as I stood in the doorway and watched her car disappear down the road, I felt the hole in my heart reopen. Overwhelmed with loneliness, I reached for my pills. When two didn't work, I took two more.

This had been going on for about a month, when one day I woke to see Marcella kneeling beside me on the kitchen floor. I managed to convince her that I had just had a dizzy spell. When she finally left me, I was gripped with fear greater than I'd ever known. Racing to the bathroom, I grabbed my bottle of pills and dumped them down the toilet. I was afraid to have them in the house, afraid I'd take too many again, afraid that next time there would be no one to help. *I may be depressed*, I thought, as I tore the prescription label into tiny bits, *but I'm not ready to die.*

I also wasn't ready for what happened next.

In a matter of hours, I became violently ill. Trembling and nauseated, I was unable to eat or sleep. At some point it occurred to me that what I was suffering was withdrawal—I had read about it somewhere. For the first time since I started taking the pills, I was faced with the alarming fact that I had become an addict, As the evening went on, I didn't care. By morning my only concern was how to get more pills.

I knew I'd have to call the doctor and tell him I had lost my prescription. I panicked at the thought. What if he suspected? What if he said no? With a trembling hand, I dialed his number. A nurse took my message. Ten minutes later she called back to say my pills were ready to be picked up.

After that, things got progressively worse. By early spring, I was popping those little pills the way others eat mints. Somehow, I managed to put on a good front for friends, and for the children when they called.

But one afternoon as I stood with pill in one hand, glass of water in the other, a small thought—like a flashing traffic signal—seemed to say, *Kaye! Stop! This is your last chance! Now or never!* There was such a sense of urgency and authority to the warning that it caused me to set the glass down.

And once again, I threw away my pills.

This time was worse than the last. By early evening, I began to shudder and shake. My head throbbed with pain. My body was wracked with fever and chills. I spent the night a pathetic heap on the bathroom floor, clinging to the toilet bowl, retching and weeping. Devilish fears and tormenting anxieties caused me to cry out loud. Finally, I couldn't take it any longer.

"Please, God," I sobbed, "help me!"

The next morning was Sunday. I woke, chilled to the bone. I showered and drank strong black coffee. I dressed and left the house. I would walk. I didn't know where, but I would walk. For some reason, I felt it was absolutely necessary that I leave the house. Besides, my husband and I had always loved our walks together. Arm in arm we often strolled across our property after an evening meal. On Sundays we walked to church.

At the sound of organ music, I was surprised to see that that was where my walk had taken me on this Sunday morning. The service was about to begin; the sound of the music seemed to draw me closer. Just as the doors closed, I slipped into a back pew. Somehow it felt good to be in church, as though that was where I was supposed to be. At the same time I felt sad, though I didn't know exactly why. Emotionally spent, physically exhausted, I was acutely aware that I had sunk just about as low as a person could go. I thought about my addiction. I wondered what my husband would think. I started to cry.

Father, I prayed—out of desperation more than anything else—*please help me. If You're really there, set me free from these pills.*

I didn't really expect an answer. It has always been my understanding that approaching God in prayer required a person to have a lot of faith. I had very little. That's why I was surprised when—as if in direct response to my prayer—a kind of quiet reassurance came to me. *"I love you,"* a voice seemed to say. *"Trust in Me, and I will take care of you."*

The pain, the anger, the emptiness I had carried for so long were not removed, but somehow my capacity for endurance and struggle was increased. It was as though my words had put me in touch with a Source of power and goodness and love unlike anything I'd ever known. And I knew that, sooner or later, I was going to be all right.

"Thank You, Father," I murmured. "Thank You."

Not that the next few months were easy. At times the struggle seemed even worse.

More than once I was thrown to my knees in prayer when tempted to call for a new prescription. And for a long while I was ashamed to admit my battle to anyone but God.

All that changed, however, when one night I read from James (5:16, NRSV). "Therefore confess your sins to one another, and pray for one another, so that you may be healed."

"Of course," I cried out loud. "Of course! You've been trying to do it all by yourself. You need the love and help that other people can give!"

The next day I confided my problem to Marcella and my children. Gaining their understanding, acceptance, and prayerful support was probably the biggest step in my healing process.

Gradually, I began to adjust to life without my husband. I began to accept lunch and dinner invitations from my friends. I rejoined women's groups at church. I signed up for volunteer work at a local hospital and nursing home. On a few occasions, I found myself with the opportunity to comfort a grieving widow.

Today, though I still miss my husband terribly, I'm living a life more fulfilling and abundant than I ever would have dreamed possible! I have learned that there is no earthly substitute for a loved one who has died. But there is God. I know now that all the time He was waiting for me with a special kind of relationship more loving and enduring than any I had ever known.

All I had to do was ask.

Restored to Life

That "special kind of relationship" with God must be steadily cultivated in-depth on a day-by-day basis. Only then can He lead us into the new, creative life He has planned for us to restore our full joy of living.

CATHERINE MARSHALL

Lesson of the Sand Dollar

BY LAVERNE PERSCHBACHER

Mike was fourteen when his dog Dugan was hit by a car. He prayed earnestly that God would spare his injured pet, but Dugan died. Then Mike turned on God much as I have seen adults do in times of trial.

He grieved terribly and spent long periods in his room. I found him there one afternoon, idly toying with a small mound of objects on his bed—a couple of round steak bones, chewed white, the little red collar and leash, and some seashells brought back from last summer's vacation.

"Mike, you have to stop this," I said. "We all miss Dugan, but we have to go on. We must accept things as they are."

"But why?" The anguish in Mike's voice was deep and real.

"This is where God comes in, Mike. I don't know why Dugan had to die, but I know God loved him as He does us and every creature on earth. Faith, Mike, is believing when you can't understand, when you can't touch or see...."

"Well, I want something I can see. Give me just one proof that I should believe—just one."

If I only could, I thought, and I looked from Mike to the small collection of memories on his bed—objects that spoke to Mike of love. Among the shells I noticed two round, flat discs, bleached white by sun and waves.

"Mike, you asked for something you could see, something tangible." Excitement put a catch in my voice. "Do you remember that when we bought those seashells, the woman told us a story about one of them?"

Mike picked up the two-inch, thin, circular shell. "She said it was called a sand dollar, and there was a legend…wait, it's on a little card she gave me." Mike got up, rummaged in his desk, and returned with a printed card. Mike began reading aloud:

There's a lovely little legend
That I would like to tell,
Of the birth and death of Jesus
Found in this lovely shell.
If you examine closely,
You'll see that you find here
Four nail holes and a fifth one
Made by a Roman's spear.
On one side the Easter lily,
Its center is the star
That appeared unto the shepherds
And led them from afar.
The Christmas poinsettia
Etched on the other side
Remind us of His birthday
Our happy Christmastide.

Now break the center open
And here you will release
The five white doves awaiting
To spread goodwill and peace.
This simple little symbol,
Christ left for you and me—
To help us spread His Gospel
Through all eternity.

It was very quiet when Mike finished reading. Then he cleared his throat.

"Five tiny white doves? It's probably just a gimmick."

"Mike, you have two sand dollars there. Let's break them open and see if they have five doves inside."

I sat down at his desk. My heart was racing as I picked up his knife. What if it really was a gimmick? My hand trembled as I plunged the knife into the hard shell.

The shell broke open, and they came tumbling out: one, two, three, four...in panic I shook the shell—and, there it was—five. Five tiny bits of white shell, each shaped like a dove in flight. Mike picked them up.

"How about that! How about that," he kept saying. Taking the knife from me he broke the other shell. Sure enough, five little white doves, all perfectly matched—formed in the depths of the ocean, countless years before, by an all-wise Creator.

I had not realized, until that moment, how my own faith had needed reaffirming too.

The light in Mike's eyes was something to see. I hope it never dims—but if it does I know that God will have another moment of revelation ready, prepared in His infinite wisdom before doubting man was even born.

Moments of Revelation

It is only in exceptional moods that we realize how wonderful are the commonest experiences of life.... At such moments one suddenly sees everything with new eyes; one feels on the brink of some great revelation. It is as if we caught a glimpse of some incredibly beautiful world that lies silently about us all the time.

J. W. N. SULLIVAN

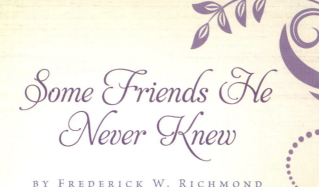

Some Friends He Never Knew

BY FREDERICK W. RICHMOND

When I flipped on the TV set after dinner one night I was looking forward to a relaxed, quiet evening, but the newscaster's first story changed everything.

Agripino Bonilla, a $68-a-week restaurant porter with ten children, had been stomped and kicked to death by three young hoodlums. It had occurred while walking just minutes away from his own door in a Brooklyn slum. He was forty-six years old.

For reasons and emotions that I have never quite understood, I impulsively reached for my coat and hurried down to get my car, aware only that I had to go to Brooklyn to see Mrs. Bonilla and her children.

I had no idea what I would say to them. All I knew was that I had to go, that I had to do something. The tragedy had struck a new chord inside me. In this brutal story there was a fundamental unfairness that cried out for justice in a voice that had never reached me before. The voice seemed to say, "We are all partly responsible for this monstrous thing."

I am fortunate in that I have an abundance of life's material things. I had tried to put this abundance to worthy use, but perhaps in ways that were impersonal. This news about Agripino Bonilla ripped through me in a very personal way. I had so much, they had so little, and now their sorrow was so great.

There was a dense crowd in front of the Bonilla tenement when I arrived. As I parked my car and walked toward the crowd, I heard a man say, "God! How could such a thing happen to these good people?"

It came to me that if I could find some answer to that question, that is what I would tell Mrs. Bonilla. I prayed that I could.

The Bonilla home was spotless. The children were all neatly dressed, quiet, stunned by their loss.

I was met at the door by a short, handsome woman with large dark eyes. I thought, *Those eyes once laughed.* Now the grief in them was deep. And they asked only one question, Why? Why?

Her greeting was courteous. She thanked me for coming. When I told her that I had not known her husband, she spoke about him quietly and with dignity: he lived for his family. This was his day off and he had gone to pay a bill. She was proud that he always paid his bills. After paying it, he went to the high school to find out how their eldest son, José, was doing. Mastering English had slowed José's schoolwork, but his father had insisted that he finish high school. Even with his meager salary, her husband had bought a fine new dictionary and had made the first payment on an encyclopedia. Now he was dead. Why?

How could such a thing happen to these good people?

I told Mrs. Bonilla that it all made no sense to me, that perhaps it was to test her faith, the faith of her children, or the stranger who should be a brother, for "a brother is born for adversity" (Proverbs 17:17 KJV).

Her eyes sought mine with understanding. She nodded. I told her I would be back, and she thanked me.

On the way home I thought, "Agripino Bonilla was either a saint or a fool." Either way, he had the kind of stubborn courage and faith I respected and admired.

But he was dead, the victim of a stupid, brutal attack that netted his mindless assailants thirty cents. In a larger sense, he had been set upon by the very despair and bitterness of the slum he sought to overcome. Could I help to achieve a victory for Agripino Bonilla so that his hopes for his family and the future need not have been in vain?

I remembered something my father liked to read to me: "If there is a poor man with you, one of your brothers, in any of your towns in your land which the LORD your God is giving you, you shall not harden your heart, nor close your hand from your poor brother" (Deuteronomy 15:7 NASB).

As a result, the Bonilla Fund was started. Proceeds would enable the family to move into a home of its own in a safe neighborhood, provide the means to educate the Bonilla children, and alleviate in some measure the financial needs of Mrs. Bonilla's later years.

Thanks to press, radio, and TV coverage, the fund flourished and many strangers became brothers. Some 1,500 letters arrived; gifts of money ranged from a few pennies, sent anonymously by people who could probably ill afford even such sums, to several substantial checks.

On the day that Agripino was to be buried, the raw air was punctuated by the usual sounds of the city: people hurrying to and from the myriad tasks that make survival possible in the slum. But added to the customary street noises was a different sound—hundreds of footfalls in muffled unison in a funeral procession. And the somber faces of the marchers were illumined by a different glow. Though it was broad daylight, hundreds of candles flickered in their hands.

This was early April, a sacred time for many people. To Christians it was the Easter season with its promise of redemption and the resurrection. To those of the Jewish faith it was the time of Passover, with its theme of deliverance from oppression.

My heart was stirred to be able to march with them. I looked into their grieving faces as they paused in their procession to pray at the spot where their neighbor was cut down, and I knew that their belief in themselves was born of a deep and abiding faith in God, just as Agripino's was. And that is why to him all things seemed possible.

A few months later we turned over the keys of a new home to Mrs. Bonilla and her children. The house has three apartments.

One would be rented to maintain the house and pay its taxes. The Fund would continue to help educate the children.

At the moment we handed over the keys to Mrs. Bonilla, I experienced a special kinship with Agripino Bonilla, a man I had never seen, but whom I knew well because in his own way he had added to the stature of many of us. Because of him we have cared and are all a little better for it.

A Kinship of Love

In whatever [God] does in the course of our lives,
He gives us, through the experience,
some power to help others.

ELISABETH ELLIOT

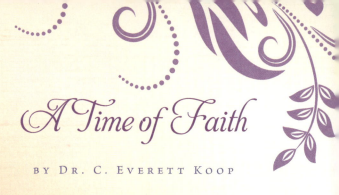

A Time of Faith

BY DR. C. EVERETT KOOP

The telephone call that came my way one June was not the sort I ordinarily receive. It was from a woman in a small town north of Philadelphia. She wanted to know if anything could be done surgically for Siamese-twin girls she had heard about who were living in the Dominican Republic.

Siamese twins. Certainly one of the most peculiar—if not horrifying—congenital defects. Once in sixty thousand births the fertilized egg fails to divide completely as it normally does when twins are conceived. When that happens, the result is the deformity named for the twins Chang and Eng born in Siam of Chinese parents early in the nineteenth century.

The first and only time I'd been involved in separating twins was years before. As I thought back on it, I remembered the restless night I had spent before the operation, troubled by frightening dreams. Fortunately, the operation was a success.

Even with the great advances in medical technology, I knew that separating Siamese twins was risky at best. Before I could give my caller an answer, though, I would need a picture of the girls. A few weeks later a photo arrived showing the twins at birth, ten months earlier. Looking at the photo, I could tell that the operation would be extremely difficult. The twins were joined at the pelvis and abdomen. I knew from my earlier experience that they shared one intestinal tract and had a crossed urinary system.

I also knew that without surgery, they were condemned to lead almost hopeless lives. When one sat up, the other would have to lie down. They would never be able to walk and their legs would shrivel from disuse.

I saw the risks in separation, but I thought it could be done successfully. When I agreed to perform the operation, things began to move swiftly. Because the twins' family was poor—I learned they lived on a farm without plumbing or electricity— money was raised by a Philadelphia church to fly the girls and their mother to the States. Children's Hospital and all my colleagues agreed to donate their services for the operation and whatever else might follow.

The twins—Clara and Alta Rodriguez—were thirteen months old when they were admitted to Children's in early September. Preparations began immediately. Though the girls had two hearts, their kidneys were linked to each other's bladders, their livers were joined, and they shared the same rectum. We would have to construct a rectum for one from a piece of the common colon. Only three of six known previous attempts to separate similarly joined Siamese twins had been successful, and one twin always had been left with a colostomy. I wanted to avoid that, to give each twin as much of a chance for a normal life as possible.

I remember the first day I saw the girls in person. They were sleeping, each holding the other's hand as if for security. Suddenly they awoke and looked up, their eyes big as oysters.

I had seen thousands of babies in my work, but there was something in those girls' eyes that seemed different. It was as if they were saying to me, "We're special." I knew then that any risk to separate them was justified. Just the thought of their going through life so grotesquely attached was overwhelmingly tragic.

Because the plan for their separation was so involved, I had little time with the twins' mother, Farida Rodriguez. She was a winsome woman who spoke no English. When she would smile faintly at me, I could sense her bewilderment. There had been so many changes in her life since she had left her husband and three sons back home in the tiny remote village of Las Auyamas, in the Dominican Republic, to bring the twins to Philadelphia.

Our preoperative sessions took a great deal of time, lasting nearly ten days and totaling several hundred man-hours of study and discussion. We had to consider everything. Though the operation would cover a number of procedures that are performed on single children many times each year at Children's, this one was different in that so many things were involved at once. It would be like a juggling act, only instead of oranges we would be handling human lives.

Our team of surgeons and anesthesiologists had to be ready for every possible contingency. For instance, what would we do if one child had a cardiac arrest, so common in separation attempts? The anesthesiology team had a tremendous responsibility. It was their job to keep the life-support systems going throughout the operation.

While we tried to anticipate all the possible problems, one that I failed to foresee was the reaction of Mrs. Rodriguez herself. Shortly before we were to perform the surgery, I found her waiting for me outside my office on the third floor. I could see she was emotionally upset. Through an interpreter I discovered that the magnitude of the surgical procedures was frightening to her. She didn't want the operation to take place if one of the girls had to die so the other could live. I tried comforting her, telling her that we would not deliberately sacrifice one to save the other, but it was possible both of them could die. As a pediatric surgeon for twenty-seven years, I had spoken to thousands of parents filled with frustration, fear, grief, and anxiety. Mrs. Rodriguez was certainly entitled to all those emotions.

I took her hands in mine and squeezed them. "Do you believe in God?" I asked.

"Yes," she answered quickly.

"So do I," I said. "I believe in the sovereignty of God and if I didn't, I couldn't take care of your children."

I've been a Christian since I was about thirty. Aside from giving me a new life, through the knowledge that Jesus Christ is my Savior, my faith has also helped me a great deal in my work. I'm able to look at tragedies—a malignant tumor in a small boy, a hole in the heart of a little girl—and see those tragedies in the light of God's will. And I can understand my own role better. If I had to go through life thinking that all the day-to-day decisions I make about patients depended on chance or on my own infallibility, I'd become very discouraged. But I know I'm not fighting a battle in the operating room all by myself.

I spoke to Mrs. Rodriguez of my faith and what it meant to me. Then I pointed to a photograph on the wall behind her.

"That was my son David," I said.

She gave me a puzzled look.

"He died six years ago, at twenty. He fell while mountain climbing in New Hampshire." I looked at the picture. A young man, so full of energy and enthusiasm, so filled with love for Christ, and yet robbed of life so early. There are times when I tell a worried or grieving parent about David. Then they know that I too have been through grief.

Mrs. Rodriguez had a simple faith in God. "I will pray," she said. "For you and for my children. It is in His hands."

On the night before the operation, wanting to be ready early for the next day, I decided to sleep at the hospital. Before retiring around midnight to a bed in a little room off my office, I went to my desk. The hospital was quiet, my office dark except for a lighted desk lamp. Framed in the window behind me, Philadelphia was asleep.

I sat down and thought of little Clara and Alta and what they were about to face. I thought again of David. Talking about him as I had done with Mrs. Rodriguez brought that bone-crushing grief to mind again. God, I knew, had taken David safely to heaven for a reason, just as He had brought Clara and Alta into this world coupled together. It was not up to me to question His reasons.

My belief that God makes no mistakes had made it possible to recover from the terrible blow of David's death, just as I knew my faith would help me tomorrow with the twins. But still, I felt the need for reassurance. I've found that faith, like a dike in a flood, needs constant reinforcement. I opened my Bible to the Psalms and read what lay before my eyes, Psalm 31. The last line seemed to repeat itself to me: "Be of good courage, and he shall strengthen your heart, all ye that hope in the LORD."

Courage. It was what I needed. God was there offering it to me. I accepted it and closed the book with renewed confidence.

It was still black outside when my call came early the next morning. I dressed quickly and walked to the OR saying, as I always do, a short prayer on the way. "Heavenly Father, please guide me in all that I do."

At 5:45 Clara and Alta were brought in and positioned on foam-rubber, wedge-shaped cushions. For the next four hours the two were readied for the operation. It was a nerve-racking period. Two full surgical teams would be working simultaneously— a total of eighteen doctors and five nurses. The tension was enormous. The world's press, radio, and television were waiting for the outcome.

At ten minutes past ten that morning, I made the first incision. After I did, things followed quickly and smoothly. When

Clara and Alta were finally separated, it was as if a great load had been lifted from my shoulders. I took a deep breath as my colleagues and I nodded to each other. The vital signs were good. We'd done it!

By the end of the operation—5:10 p.m.—I was drained but exhilarated. I immediately relayed the good news to Mrs. Rodriguez. She responded by saying—to my embarrassment— "There are two gods, one in heaven and one in Philadelphia." I laughed, but I knew whom she should really thank.

Later that evening, I went to the infant intensive-care unit where Clara and Alta were confined. I watched their tiny figures dwarfed by the respirators that breathed for them and the tubes and consoles that monitored their every bodily function. How peaceful they looked sleeping their first night as separate little girls. Then I noticed that Clara, still alongside her sister, had locked her hand snugly in Alta's. They were sleeping the same way they had when they were one.

Something touched me inside. God, I knew, was in that room, telling those two children that everything was all right, just as He had let me know the night before.

As I stared down at Clara and Alta I realized how very special they were. They were a true miracle of medical science. Yet there before me was another kind of miracle—that of God's love. He had cared enough to give us the skills to change one helpless form into two beautiful people.

In His Hands

So do not fear, for I am with you;
do not be dismayed, for I am your God.
I will strengthen you and help you;
I will uphold you with my righteous right hand.

ISAIAH 41:10 NIV

Alligator!

BY KERMIT GEORGE

The July morning was hot, sticky, sweltering. Wiping the sweat from my brow, I leaned my 10-speed bicycle against a tree and gazed out at the lake. Squirrels chattered from the treetops, rabbits skirted through the underbrush, toads croaked down by the shore. Duchess, my black Doberman pinscher, scampered into the water. How I wished I myself could be that carefree.

This was the first free moment I'd had in a week and I couldn't get business worries out of my head. As an electrical engineer, I was employed by SRI International, a government contractor for Eglin Air Force Base across the Florida border. Besides that, I had my own business at home as a surveyor. Between the two jobs I worked seven days a week, fourteen hours a day. I had to, I felt; I was deep in debt from heavy losses in the cattle market.

I looked longingly at the lake. The water was so peaceful and calm. Open Pond, as it was called, was part of Conecuh National Forest. I knew the area well. My grandparents farmed nearby, and as a boy I often visited. How much simpler life was back in those days. My mama and grandma took me to church and taught me my prayers. "Whenever you're in trouble," Mama had said, "just call on the Lord for help."

Now I was in more trouble than I cared to admit, but I'd long since stopped praying. I figured I could solve all my problems on my own; I didn't need help. For the time being I just wanted to escape—explore the woods or take a dip in the lake.

Duchess was splashing in the water and tugging at a stick. "Good girl," I called. I could smell bacon frying at a campground in the distance. I could see two fishermen in a skiff across the lake. In the July heat the water was irresistible.

On an impulse I kicked off my tennis shoes. I tossed my T-shirt over the bicycle's handlebars and walked down the sloping sand. At the water's edge I called playfully to Duchess. "Over here, girl." She bounded toward me and jumped on my chest. I rubbed her neck and we tusseled for a while in the shallow water. Then she was ready to get out.

"Go wait on shore for me," I told her, gesturing toward the beach. She ambled away, panting, wagging her tail. I walked out to deeper water.

The hot sun glared on the lake. The air was still. With only my head above water, I stretched my arms out and relaxed. At last I was at peace.

Suddenly there was a wild thrashing in the water as something grabbed hold of my outstretched arm and wrenched it with a violent jerk. An alligator! I tried to pull free, but I couldn't. I twisted and turned, but I was no match for the creature's overwhelming strength. I felt the breath being sucked out of me as the alligator pulled me beneath the surface of the water and dragged me against the bottom.

I'm going to be eaten alive, I thought, *or I'm going to drown.* My mind was going fuzzy.

And then suddenly, as suddenly as it had attacked, the alligator let go. I dug my toes in the sand and tried to stand; I was almost too weak. Duchess stared at me from the shore; she seemed miles away. *I've got to stay conscious,* I told myself. Surprised to be alive, I staggered through the murky water. I looked down.

My right arm was gone.

"My God, my God," I cried. My eyes blurred. Somehow I dragged myself to the shore.

"Help! Help!" I called. With all the strength I could muster, I waved my left arm in the direction of the fishermen. Duchess barked.

"Help me, please."

No response.

A long sliver of skin dangled just a few inches below my shoulder joint. My heart was beating fast and my breath was short. I knew I had to lie down to avoid going into shock. I collapsed in the sand.

After a few minutes I looked back up, only to see the boat going away from me, trying to escape the alligator. Now there seemed no hope. Muddled thoughts crept in and out of my mind. I could see myself as a boy, going to church with Mama. I could hear her reminding me to say my prayers. "Remember, when you're in trouble, turn to God."

Suddenly Duchess started barking. I looked up and saw the fishermen beaching the skiff, but Duchess wouldn't let them come near. I called her to me, and one of them, a white-haired gentleman, approached and looked down at me in disbelief.

"Do something," I said, "or I'm going to die." The man paused. "Make a compress," I suggested. He quickly took off his shirt, wadded it up and held it against the wound.

"Sir, are you a Christian?" I asked.

"Yes. Yes, I am," he answered.

"Will you pray for me?"

"Yes," the fisherman said. And then he began. "God, be with this man," he prayed. "Comfort him, watch over him. He needs You, God." And as this good man prayed for me, I did feel comforted.

Gradually a small crowd gathered. Finally someone came in a green pickup truck. Strong, capable hands lifted me onto the hot metal bed of the truck. As the truck jerked forward, I fought slipping into unconsciousness, and I thanked God I was alive.

First they took me to the medical center in Andalusia, Alabama. I was stabilized there and then transfered to the University of South Alabama Medical Center in Mobile. A man in antiseptic white said I would be there at least three weeks and that it would probably take three or four operations to clear the wound of infections.

"An alligator's mouth harbors a tremendous amount of bacteria," he explained.

Another man told me the alligator had been shot. The animal measured 12 feet long and weighed 500 pounds.

After my visitors left, I lay in bed pondering, but not about the alligator. I kept thinking of the fisherman and the way he'd prayed for me. With him I had acknowledged my need for prayer through Christ for the first time in years. Now I knew what Mama had meant.

"From now on, God, I'm not going to wait for trouble to call on You," I said half out loud.

I was released from the hospital eight days later; the infections the doctors had feared never materialized. Now came the struggle of putting my life back together. I had to relearn so much—getting dressed, eating meals, driving a car. With only my left hand I had to resume a profession that depends on writing and measuring with exactitude. And yet I didn't worry anymore.

Four years have passed since then. I continue my engineering business, but now I take time to attend church regularly and to serve others through a prison ministry. I have found peace in my life and a new purpose.

Purpose and Meaning

I believe that nothing
that happens to me is meaningless,
and that it is good for us all that it should be so,
even if it runs counter to our own wishes.
As I see it, I'm here for some purpose,
and I only hope I may fulfill it.

DIETRICH BONHOEFFER

Annie's Kitchen

BY ANNIE LONARDO

F our months after my husband's funeral and I still couldn't believe my Bob was gone. I wandered through our house, unable to do anything but cry. Every room was bursting with memories. I stood in the kitchen, our favorite spot, wiping my cheeks. I could almost see him standing by the stove while I cooked, ready to do his job—testing the macaroni. "It'll be perfect in another half-minute," he'd say, shooting me a smile, his deep brown eyes crinkling. I turned away, only to find my gaze settling on a portrait of us hanging nearby, yet another painful reminder of my loss.

That night, in bed, I felt so lonely and hopeless, I begged God, "Take me! My life means nothing without Bob. What am I supposed to do now?"

Fifty-four years we'd been together. We met in Providence, Rhode Island, when I was still in high school. We both came from tight-knit Italian families. My parents didn't allow me to date. But there was something special about Bob, a warmth that made me feel at home. A childhood bout of polio left him with a limp and a leg brace, but he never let that get him down. I would slip out at night and meet him at the Moose Head diner, where we fell in love over fifty-cent cups of hot cocoa. Eventually, I worked up the nerve to introduce him to my family. It didn't take long for them to love him too.

After we married, Bob studied at New York University and became an orthotist—designing splints and braces for folks like him. We opened our own business. Bob worked with the patients; I kept the books and arranged fittings.

We were a great team at home too. I loved to cook and Bob loved to eat! "Honey, you can cover anything in red gravy and I'll eat it," he'd joke. Bob made me feel like I made the best food in the world.

We had six children and held tight to the traditions passed down from our families. Meals were for bonding, a time for all of us to be together. Weeknights I made everything from prosciutto with melon for an antipasto and braciola or chicken Marsala with boiled potatoes and salad drizzled with olive oil for supper. Sundays were for meatballs. I'd roll a hundred or more before church, my daughters helping me just like I used to help my mom. To us, food was love.

The kids grew up and started their own families. Bob and I retired to Florida. After fifty years of marriage we still had candlelit dinners every night. We'd laugh and make little lists of things we wanted to do, movies to see. With Bob, there was always something to look forward to.

But then everything changed. Bob had a cough that just wouldn't quit. It turned out to be stage four lung cancer. Doctors gave Bob four months to live.

He made it three.

Now here I was, all alone, crying myself to sleep, my life feeling as empty as the house we once shared. The plea I made to God was still on my mind when I woke up the next morning: what am I supposed to do now?

Okay, I asked myself, *what do I like to do?* Cook, of course. But who would I cook for? I called our pastor. He suggested I make a welcome-home dinner for a group returning from a mission trip. At least it would keep me busy.

I cooked our family classics—stuffed peppers, pizza, sausage and meatballs. The food was a hit. Soon I was making eggplant for neighbors, stuffed shells for high-school graduations, and chicken cutlets for children's parties. Cooking for people dimmed my grief a little, but still, something was missing. *Lord, You're going to have to knock me on my head and let me know what more I can do.*

An idea hit me faster than I could roll a meatball. Why not truly share what I loved and not only give people a taste of my food but also teach them to make it for themselves? I called my daughter, Kathy, who lived nearby. We rounded up friends and neighbors, photocopied recipes, bought name tags. Within a few days, I had ten women standing in my kitchen. Kathy started the class by reading from Jeremiah. "For I know the plans I have for you," declares the Lord. "Plans to prosper you and not to harm you, plans to give you hope and a future" (29:11 NIV). At the end of the evening, everyone wanted to know what we'd be cooking in our next class. "Annie's Apron Strings" was born.

My girls (that's what I call my students) gather in my kitchen each Monday evening. We cook, we laugh, we eat! And I tell them all about Bob. Every recipe seems to lead me back to a story about our years together. I love knowing that his favorite recipes live on, and I think Bob would be happy to know that our house—especially our kitchen—is full of life again.

So far, I've taught more than one hundred of my girls and I donate their class fees (ten dollars a week) to help needy folks in town. It's the perfect recipe for overcoming my grief, a recipe that gives me new hope and a future and helps others find one too.

Recipe for Hope

Start with a measure of faith.
Blend in a scoop of kindness.
Stir in the encouragement of family and friends.
Sprinkle in the sweetness of memories.
Bake in the sunshine of God's love
Until hope overflows the pan.

The Pilot's Daughter

BY CAROLINE OGONOWSKI

I quietly closed the door of my freshman dorm room behind me at Boston College, but not before I glanced back at the photo of Dad and me. The one of me as a girl sitting on his lap in the cockpit of a 767.

I wish you were here, Dad, I thought as I walked down the hall from my room. *I wish you were here to help me figure all this out.*

I was glad my new roommate was still asleep. "I'm going to be gone tomorrow, at a family event," I'd told her the night before, and she'd thankfully been totally disinterested. It was as if September 11 wasn't even on her mind. I suppose I shouldn't have been surprised. Even the front page of the newspaper was focused on Hurricane Katrina.

How quickly we forget, I thought. It seemed too soon. But I'd been glad to delay the inevitable talk with my roommate. I wasn't ready to see the shock in her eyes, to hear how sorry she felt for me, to be the victim—again.

How do you tell someone that your dad was the pilot on Flight 11, the first plane that terrorists flew into the World Trade Center? For four years now I'd prayed that I'd be able to figure out where 9/11 fit into my life. But as a freshman starting high school on that terrible day, I never got a chance to introduce myself before everyone thought they knew who I was. I watched as kids furtively glanced at me and then quickly looked away. The "9/11 girl." I didn't want to be defined by a tragedy, yet I wanted to honor Dad. He too was more than just the person he was on that terrible day. I wanted to be my own person.

I hoped to find my identity starting college. Isn't that what kids are meant to do in college? Find themselves? But once again the date loomed: September 11. Now, if I was going to make a clean start, I had to get to the memorial service without anyone on campus making a big deal about it.

Outside my dorm I spotted the car with my mother and two sisters. I jumped in so we could make the short drive to Boston's Public Garden.

Slouched in the backseat, I thought about the memorial services I'd attended in the last four years. There had been so many that they were starting to fade into one another. "We will always remember," politicians often said. But each year there was more I couldn't recall. The pain was less, but even that seemed sad, in a different kind of way. How am I supposed to feel? What would Dad want me to remember?

Two years before on 9/11 we had come to BC to dedicate a labyrinth in memory of the twenty-two alumni killed. Mom graduated from BC, class of '76, so a portion of the memorial honored Dad. I too had picked BC by then. A speaker told how the labyrinth was a Christian symbol of the twists and turns of life's journey. Somehow it was comforting to know it would be there for me. *God,* I prayed, *help me find the path to take in my life.* Yet as Mom turned into the Public Garden I felt so lost.

We joined the hundreds of others already there. Sitting near the front I craned my neck. The crowd seemed a bit smaller each year. "I'm glad we're here," I told Mom. "Already you can tell this is just another day for some people. They've stopped coming. I don't want people to forget 9/11—or Dad."

"I understand, honey," she said. "But you can't take that burden all on yourself. Besides, there are lots of ways to honor someone."

At 8:40 a.m. the mayor solemnly laid a wreath of remembrance. Then five minutes later we paused for a moment of silence, just as the entire world had stopped that Tuesday morning. Closing my eyes, I relived the day, like I had so many times before:

Dad leaving our 150-acre farm early, before I was awake, to pilot an 8 a.m. flight from Logan Airport to LA...the announcement as school was starting...a counselor coming to take me out of class...a blur—people at the house crying and hugging, the memorial services, the media—that lasted for weeks...then going back to school, my identity sealed: The Pilot's Daughter.

The service ended and we walked back to the car. I heard Mom's words again, about finding other ways to honor Dad. On the drive back to the campus I said, "It's funny. Most of the time when I think of Dad it's not about him as a pilot at all. What I see is him driving the tractor at home and playing with us kids. That's who he really was, a farmer and a dad."

"You're right," Mom said. "The farm is where he felt most at home. It's really where he felt closest to God. He loved everything about farming. He loved the feeling that he was giving something back, but he got so much out of it."

In front of my dorm building I gave everyone a hug, especially Mom. "I miss Dad so much," I whispered to her.

"Me too," Mom said. "He would be so proud of you."

Back in my room I was relieved to see my roommate was out. I lay on my bed staring at the ceiling. I remembered how my father had mentored immigrant farmers, not only working with them and giving advice but sharing his land for them to grow their native crops. Dad, a former transport pilot in Vietnam, chose to mentor farmers from Southeast Asia. He threw himself into a federal support program for immigrant farmers, so much so that, when he was killed, it was named in his honor. Mom was right. One of Dad's jobs was flying jets, but his life was about helping others. He was an amazing guy. He was so much more than just one of the hijacked pilots on 9/11.

I was so lost in thought I barely noticed when my roommate walked in the door.

"How was the thing you went to?" my roommate said. Was she looking at me funny, or was it just me?

"It was fine," I said, scrambling to get my guard up. "How's your day been?"

"It's been good," she said, but her mouth kind of twitched, like there was something else she wanted to say. "I was watching TV this morning and I saw you at the memorial service. Was your dad the pilot on Flight 11? I wish I had known."

I'd tried so hard to avoid this conversation. With a sigh I said, "It's just a hard thing to talk about. I was really hoping to get to know you better first. And I wanted you to get to know me."

I could see she was trying to think of what to say. "I understand," she said. "It was just kind of shocking to see my roommate on TV. Listen, the reason why I came back is because I've been out with some other students collecting money for Hurricane Katrina victims. Want to help?"

Helping others. That's what Dad was all about. What better way to honor him today! Would it help with these feelings?

"Sure," I said. "You don't know how great that sounds." I headed out with her.

After some orientation we all spread across campus. I walked up to a student and introduced myself. "Hi, my name is Caroline. I'm a freshman here and I'm collecting money for people hurt by the hurricane. Would you be willing to help?"

"Sure," he said, digging five dollars out of his jeans. "I'd love to do something. Maybe I'll see you around campus."

By evening I'd raised over a hundred dollars. Heading across campus, I thought about the afternoon. It left me with a kind of tingling feeling inside. For years it had been me on the receiving end of people's sympathy. It was well-meant sympathy, but it was also a kind of wall, a 9/11 wall. Now here I was doing something to help other people hurt by senseless tragedy. I had met dozens of new people, none of whom saw me as anything but a college student. It felt good. Actually, it felt incredible.

I was walking back to the dorm when I saw the labyrinth on my left. I walked over to it. At the entrance I again read the verse inscribed there, from Isaiah, one of Dad's favorites. "They that hope in the Lord will renew their strength, they will soar as with eagles' wings...."

Dad was always happiest when he was doing something for others, when he was working for a common good. It was as if I were looking down a long row of a freshly plowed field, my father's tractor far in the distance. I realized how I could best honor Dad's memory, following a row already tilled for me. Could I find my identity within 9/11? Could it actually hold the seeds for who I wanted to be in life? It was hard to believe.

Pulling out my cell phone I called Mom. "I've been thinking about Dad a lot today, about 9/11 and who I want to be. I think I partially know the answer. I'd like to do work where I'm helping other people, people who have been in tragedies."

Mom was silent for a moment. Then she said, "Caroline, I think that's wonderful. It's funny because even when you were a little girl that's how your dad and I saw you. I remember when you were only two years old and I was pregnant with your sister you put a blanket around me when I wasn't feeling well. You've always been such a caring person. Just like your father."

When I hung up the phone there was that tingling feeling again.

I graduated, and as another school year begins, I'm preparing to earn a master's in counseling psychology at Boston College, in hopes of working with children dealing with trauma. For the last four years I've volunteered for the Red Cross, urging college students to give blood. I'm becoming my own person, the one my dad would have wanted me to be.

Some years on September 11 our family will gather at the farm for a more private ceremony. Far from the roar of the city, it's not a place that stirs memories of 9/11. But I've learned that's okay. It's the perfect spot for me to honor a farmer, a pilot, my dad, a caring man, whose love guides me to this day.

A Legacy of Giving

Give, and it will be given to you. A good measure, pressed down, shaken together and running over, will be poured into your lap. For with the measure you use, it will be measured to you.

LUKE 6:38 NIV

Courage for Sad Times

BY LEONORA WOOD

At age ninety-two, I have lived long past the biblical span of allotted years. And, as others who share my age know, it has its mixed blessings. I have lived long enough to meet and enjoy eight great-grandchildren, to see the beauty of countless sunsets and green leafings of springs. And I have grieved over the deaths of loved ones, often—too often— before their time. I have traveled the road of life long enough to know that it is neither smooth nor straight, and though I am never really ready for its sudden turns, I am confident about how I should handle them when they come.

One March my sixty-eight-year-old daughter, Catherine Marshall LeSourd, went into the hospital for some blood tests. I was not prepared for the news telling me that she had died. I was stunned, shattered. I had already lost a husband, my son Bob, my son-in-law Peter Marshall, two little great-grand-children, and other dear ones. Losing Catherine seemed too much to bear.

But as I sat at the window in my house in Florida weeping and praying, it was as if the Lord came to me. He seemed to be saying: *"Don't cry. Catherine is with Me and she is happy."* And just as I was worrying about how I would face the emptiness of a world without this beautiful, caring daughter, He gave me some directions. *"You must return to your farm in Virginia and help build My church."*

It was almost an audible voice and I knew it was my Lord. I also knew what He was telling me to do. Building a church near my Virginia home of Evergreen Farm had long been a dream. And if I wondered how I could possibly do what He was so clearly telling me to do, I did not wonder long. *"Fear not,"* He was saying to me once more, *"I will help thee."*

As I sat by the window in Florida that March morning, my mind drifted back seventy-three years to a snowy afternoon in a tiny mountain town where those words of the Lord had their first real meaning for me.

I had volunteered to teach in a mission school up in the Great Smoky Mountains, an adventure that later inspired Catherine's novel *Christy*. When I hugged my father good-bye in the grimy Asheville railroad station on that winter morning, he was wiping his eyes. He felt I was too young and inexperienced. I was only eighteen. But he did not try to talk me out of it. Instead, he gave me courage. "Take these words with you," he said. "Take them to heart. They are from Isaiah 41:13: 'For I the LORD thy God will hold thy right hand, saying unto thee, Fear not; I will help thee.' "

I whispered those words as I waved through the coach window until Papa was lost in the steam and smoke.

It was snowing even harder when I finally stepped off the train at the little way station of Del Rio, Tennessee, expecting someone to meet me. But the snow-drifted platform was empty. I creaked open the door and hesitantly approached a man in a green eyeshade with muttonchop whiskers who was tapping a telegraph key.

Turning to me, he scratched his head and said: "Nope, nobody from the mission's been here." Then, looking at me closer through wire-rimmed glasses, he added, "But, I'll tell you, Miss, Mrs. Bernet across the way keeps boarders; you might be more comfortable there."

After picking my way across the tracks through the deepening snow, I knocked on Mrs. Bernet's paint-cracked door. It was pulled back by a heavy woman with a gray bun who ushered me in.

The aroma of pot roast filled the hall and she kindly invited me to join the others for dinner.

"What are you doing here in Del Rio?" she asked as I hung up my coat.

"I am going to teach at the Ebenezer mission school," I said.

She stared at me, hands on hips.

"You know what my advice is, little girl?"

"No," I replied, trembling.

"Have you ever lived where you wash clothes in a tub an' beat 'em with a stick?" She threw a look out the snow-encrusted window. "It's rough livin' up in those hills. My advice to you, little girl, is to get right back on the next train and go home."

I was mortified. Did I look that vulnerable? For a moment I wavered. Perhaps she was right. Home now seemed so safe and warm. And my parents would welcome me back.

"Fear not," came the words, *"I will help thee."*

I knew instinctively that the Lord's promise was not for those who gave up, but for those who forged ahead. Just as He guided the Israelites as they left Egypt to work their way through the wilderness, I knew He would guide me.

I looked up at the landlady and tried to keep my voice steady. "Mrs. Bernet, all I want to do is get out to the mission in the morning."

She pursed her lips, then smiled, seeing, I suppose, that I meant business. The next morning she took me to the little post office where I met the mail delivery man.

"You can walk with me up to the mission, if you like," he said, pulling on his boots. "It's seven miles," he grunted.

The powdery snow was deep, but I trudged along with him carrying my bag.

It took all morning working our way along wind-whipped rocky ridges and slogging through shadowy hollows, but finally we reached the Ebenezer mission.

The next day I was teaching in its one-room school, where I found the mountain children bright and inquisitive. Their minds were keen and they wanted to learn. But I soon found myself in over my head.

The problem was Noah. I had been warned about him from the start. Almost my age but towering over me, he was the class bully. Word was he'd once threatened a teacher with a knife.

Things came to a head during math class. I was demonstrating fractions on the blackboard when I kept being interrupted by a *click-bang, click-bong*. It was Noah; he was leering at me.

"Noah," I said levelly, "please stop making that noise."

He smirked and the click-banging continued.

Caution dictated that I ignore him. But I knew this was a watershed; either I would be in charge or he would run things.

"Fear not, I will help thee."

I walked to Noah's desk. "Noah," I said firmly, "I asked you to stop."

He glared at me, surged up from behind his desk, and snarled: "I'll stop when I d—well get ready!"

In that instant, I did what I believe Providence wanted me to do. I hauled off and slapped his cheek with all my might.

The husky youth stared at me wide-eyed.

Breathing hard, I ordered him to settle in his seat and stay there. He sulked the rest of the day.

That evening as dusk darkened the piney woods, I happened to glance out one of the mission's wavery-glass windows to see Noah and his father marching up the path. His father was a giant, almost as tall as a corncrib, with the shoulders of an ox.

"Now what?" I wondered.

Their boots clumped on the porch and a fist pounded the door. I drew it back and with a tremulous voice invited them in.

Noah's father shook his hairy head when I offered a chair. "What I got to say won't take much time," he growled. Then, his eyes glinting like the edge of a new-honed ax, he said: "Miss Whitaker, I have just come to thank you for what you did for Noah this morning. You are the first teacher that has ever controlled him." He turned and glared at his son, who stood staring at the floor, then looked back at me. "Now, maybe you can pound some sense into his thick head."

Well, Noah and I got along fine after that and he went on to become a good student.

A year later, I came to another turn in the road. John Wood, a handsome young mission preacher with brown eyes and black hair, asked me to marry him.

My new husband's first pastorate was the Meadow Creek Presbyterian Church in the Tennessee foothills. After a wonderful three years there, he was called to the little town of Umatilla, Florida, where we lived in a small rented house. The church wanted us to have a manse, and though John, a good carpenter, offered to build it, we needed materials.

At that time the famous William Jennings Bryan, who ran three times for the presidency, was in the area. Someone suggested that if we could get him to speak, we could count on a sizable collection. Well, I didn't know how to handle something big like that, and I was daunted by the prospect, so I put it all in God's hands.

"Fear not, I will help thee."

I went to Ocala, a big town nearby, where the Great Commoner was speaking. As I was registering at the hotel, who should come to the desk but the tall, dignified Mr. Bryan and his entourage. I just turned, introduced myself, and invited him to speak at our church.

He smiled, bowed, and said: "I'll be at your house Friday, ma'am, for chicken dinner." Mr. Bryan was a man who dearly loved his victuals. Well, come he did and he was just wonderful. They didn't call him the Silver-Tongued Orator for nothing. He spoke right to my heart that hot afternoon when he said that if we really try to do the right thing, the circumstances of life tend to work together to promote the very thing we're trying to accomplish. As the Bible says, "All things work together for good for those who love God" (Romans 8:28).

Mr. Bryan also enjoyed my fried chicken and we did have a good offering that helped us get the building materials. John worked all summer building that manse.

Several years later, John's health disintegrated; one Sunday morning he fainted right in the pulpit. He had to resign. Once again I found myself asking for God's help in meeting a new turn in the road.

And He did. John recovered and we were called to Canton, Mississippi. It was difficult leaving a place where we had done much in helping build up a church. But God was with us in Canton, and John pastored there for three years. It was a bigger responsibility for him and a real growing period for both of us.

Through John's fifty years in the ministry we had responsibility for fifteen churches and lived in seven different states. Finally, at age seventy, John retired and we moved to Evergreen Farm in the little Quaker hamlet of Lincoln, Virginia. Catherine had bought Evergreen for us after her book *A Man Called Peter* was such a success. It was a wonderful place for us; John was so happy fixing it up. However, he had a heart condition and as time went by had to take it easy. So when Catherine wanted to take us with her on a trip to California, I felt uneasy. I just couldn't decide whether we should go or not.

One afternoon, John had gone to our little country post office/general store to pick up our mail; he always liked visiting there, talking with the local men and the proprietors, Asa Moore Janney and his wife, Arlene, the postmistress. I was alone in the house resting, when the front door opened and our family doctor stepped in. He wore his white coat and I wondered why. We talked for a bit and then I asked him.

"Dr. Oliver, I have a problem and a question. Catherine wants us to go with her to California and I just have a strong feeling that John shouldn't be away from home right now."

Dr. Oliver stared at the floor for a moment, then at me. "Well," he said quietly and kindly, "your problem is solved and your question is answered. He's gone."

The postmistress had called Dr. Oliver. My husband had been in the post office sitting in a chair talking and he just went to sleep. It was a heart attack.

For a long time, it seemed unreal. I felt that I might soon wake up and find it was all just a bad dream. My children gathered around me. And as I looked at them, it soon became clear that they had all suffered their own sorrows and tragedies. They needed to be sustained. They needed the scraps of wisdom I had collected along the way.

And so it was that I decided what course to take. I reached out to the Lord, my God, and let Him take my right hand.

"Fear not," said the Lord, *"I will help thee."*

Little by little the people I loved have slipped away. Peter Christopher, an infant great-grandson—my grandson Peter John Marshall's child—died. Peter's infant daughter, Amy Catherine, died five years later. And another five years later, Bob, my only son, died at the age of fifty-three. And then Bob's son, twenty-eight-year-old Johnny Wood, died suddenly and tragically. These are the hardest times, especially when those who are younger than you take their leave, and there are times when I forget and permit myself to think that I am in the midst of death. But this is not so. It is life that surrounds me. Life. Life that is meant to be lived, its riches to be extracted. It is no different now than the day I stood in the snow in Del Rio determined not to give up and go home. No, the Lord's promise is not for those who give up, but for those who forge ahead.

I am back in Virginia doing what I have been doing for years here at Evergreen, busy with the day-to-day details of running a farm, hosting the many visitors who come here, fellowshipping with family in counseling and prayer, teaching my regular Tuesday-morning Bible study for the ladies. And, as He directed me that morning after Catherine died, helping to build His church. Already, a little congregation has gathered to fill it.

I hold a vision of it, white frame and steeple with chimes ringing out over the countryside.

Oh, it will take some steps to help bring it about. And, as always, I don't know what the road ahead holds for me. But though my feet aren't steady and my vision is dim, I will walk on down it, secure in the promise given me seventy-three years ago that He will hold my right hand and steady me with His assurance: *"Fear not; I will help thee."*

It's a promise He has always kept.

Promises Kept

God is the God of promise. He keeps His word, even when that seems impossible; even when the circumstances seem to point to the opposite.

COLIN URQUHART

The Reassurance

BY NANCY L. COLE

Amee was my daughter, and she died in a Connecticut hospital at the age of twenty-two. It was her thirteenth hospitalization in six years, mostly for emotional reasons and substance abuse. Amee had been driven to try every modern-day trap for today's young people: drugs, alcohol, destructive relationships. Ironically, she died not by her own hand—for she'd tried that too—but from the toxic effects of a hospital drug improperly monitored. For two weeks she lingered in a coma, then she was gone.

Gone. This lovely daughter of mine who had been so bright and talented, a gifted singer and dancer, and, like me, an artist. Amee's father and I were divorced about the time she entered her teens. And until that time, I thought her upbringing had been a happy one. We were, after all, a fairly normal American family—Sundays at church, Fourth-of-July kind of values. Then Amee began to change.

Amee started wearing heavy makeup. She began smoking pot. The partying began, and she was out until all hours or not coming home at all. She didn't respond to discipline. Our relationship broke down. Eventually, the deep depressions, and the hospitals.

After Amee died, yes, of course, I blamed myself, but my grief was deeper than that. I was worried. I knew she'd been so self-destructive. When a spiritual counselor suggested that because of her lifestyle Amee might not have gone to heaven, I became inconsolable. I couldn't imagine her being in any more hell than she already had been.

People tried to help me. My mother listened with a mother's love. My two best friends let me cry and cry. But the months lengthened into one...two...three years.

I sought and found others like myself at Compassionate Friends, a national fellowship of adults who have lost children by death. They didn't think it odd when I told them some of the crazy things I'd done. Like how I'd buried my face in her clothes, trying to catch a scent of my daughter. Nor did they blink when I described how I'd come across a wad of Amee's chewing gum stuck on one of her record albums: without hesitating, I'd popped it into my mouth, desperate to recapture some essence of her.

But more than anything else, I wanted to know where Amee was. I could not rest until I knew she was safe with God.

And during this long period of grieving I kept thinking about the books: seven thick art books that Amee had filled and carried around with her wherever she went. I knew that during her hospital stays they were her closest companions and her own form of therapy. At first after Amee's death I had hesitated even opening their covers, but then I did, and soon I was drawn into Amee's sensitive, dark-and-bright, searching-and-struggling innermost life. I'd encouraged her with her art for years. But now the pages of sayings, quotations, and diary-like thoughts, all set down in delicate calligraphy and interspersed with drawings of flowers, butterflies, and beautiful young girls, seemed entirely new. They showed me Amee in an illuminated way after death that I could not see when she was alive. I was stunned by Amee's despair and yet was moved by her hunger for the comfort of God's love.

"I'll be twenty-one this month," she wrote on one page, "another birthday celebrated in a mental institution. Each one sorrow-filled, me wanting to cry out in grief. It's never-ending, this painful fear. When does it go away?"

And on another page: "I am starving, starving. I feel alone, so desperately alone. I wish I could hand my feelings over to someone else—just for a day because they couldn't tolerate them any longer. But then that person would be on my side; it would no longer be me against the world."

Again and again I'd pull out Amee's books from beneath my bed, grieved by the despair I read in their pages, yet hoping, searching for some clue that would relieve my agony, that would give me that final assurance that, yes, Amee was okay, safe in heaven. And the more I read, the more it seemed that Amee was talking to me from those books. I was feeling her suffering. I was crying with her, crying for the girls she drew who were never without tears.

One afternoon, however, I was sitting with one of Amee's books in hand, just thinking about her, when I glanced at a drawing inside the back cover. Somehow I hadn't noticed it before. Amee had drawn another of her young women, but this one was different. There were no tears. And alongside was her penciled Scripture reference: "Revelation 21:4: 'And God will wipe away every tear from their eyes.'" Now I began to go back and seek out other samples of a more optimistic Amee, especially in the book she began while living at a Christ-centered residential facility for troubled youth. "I'm born again," she lettered on the opening page.

"The soul can rise from the earth into the sky," Amee wrote one day, "like a bird aware of its freedom." And from one of her worst times I found this: "God will come...I will never give up. No, I've fought too long and hard." Or the full page of lettering: "Deep within there cometh peace. A child of His I am."

I wanted to believe it was true. Was it? Even though she had stumbled and fallen again and again after that?

I felt something new stirring within me. It was hope. But hope is expectation. I wanted something more. Was this a break-through? Was something more coming?

There was. And it came from Amee's father, who lived nearby. Bob had been a loving father, just as I had been a loving mother; sorrow had spared neither of us. And it happened that one day Bob experienced something that changed us both.

He was out shopping, only faintly aware of the music being piped throughout the mall, until he heard a Crosby, Stills and Nash song, "Sweet Judy Blue Eyes." Bob stopped. That had been one of Amee's favorites. He listened to the lyrics about voices and moonlight, then "...She's so free. How can you catch the sparrow?" To him, the lyrics were confusing. He wondered what meaning they might have had for Amee.

Bob drove to his home, a summer cottage with high cathedral ceilings. No sooner had he entered than he heard an odd sound, a thap-thapping. He looked up to see a little bird trapped inside the house, frantically flying against a window in its efforts to get out. Bob went for a stepladder, climbed up, and soon was holding the trembling creature in his hands. Carefully he climbed down and headed outside, where he paused, then slowly opened his hands. The bird fluttered out and up and into the sky.

"She's so free," Bob said aloud, repeating the words of the song Amee had loved. Then the other words came to mind, "How can you catch the sparrow?" At that instant Bob realized that the bird he had just let go free was a sparrow.

For a moment Bob stood motionless, looking up into the now-empty sky. "Good-bye, Amee. Good-bye, little bird," he said softly. Then he looked down into his still-cupped hands. There lay two tiny tail feathers. And at once, without knowing how he knew, he was sure that one was for him, one for me.

And so it was. But there was even more to the story of the sparrow, for when I received my feather, I went to press it in one of Amee's art books for safekeeping. I picked up the first book I could put my hand on and opened it. There before me was a design in blue curlicues over which Amee had superimposed the words "I wish I was a tiny sparrow sheltered in God's hands."

There it was, finally: the reassurance I had been seeking. The hope Amee's books had kindled in me was now fulfilled. Fulfilled by a fragile series of events that I knew, by faith, had been strung together by a loving Creator.

I could be at peace now. Amee was with God, like a frightened, troubled little sparrow sheltered at last in His loving hands.

Sheltering Arms

The eternal God is your refuge,
and underneath are the everlasting arms.

DEUTERONOMY 33:27 NIV

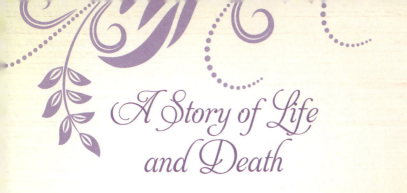

A Story of Life and Death

BY JENNY WADE

My friend Tim [not his real name] died at the age of forty-four. I'd known him for six years, ever since I went to work in Dallas, Texas, for a large corporation involved in communications technology. I liked him instantly, and liked him even more as I got to know him. His faith, his honesty, his devotion to his family—these qualities drew me to him. Tim's death changed the way I look at my life.

At the time I met Tim, I was an ambitious twenty-eight-year-old woman who'd cracked the upper-management echelon in a highly competitive, traditionally male field. I worked hard. My career meant an awful lot to me. Because I was a woman, I always felt I had to work a little harder, a little longer to get the respect and success I wanted. Tim helped put things in perspective for me.

I remember once we were pushing hard on a project. Calvin, the vice president of our division, let it be known that he expected us to work through the weekend if necessary. That didn't bother me. But one day during a project conference, Tim spoke up.

"Cal, I know how important this thing is for the company, but I promised my daughter Terry I'd help her out with a bake sale Saturday at our church. I can't go back on my word. We'll have to find time during the week to get caught up."

Tim found time—coming in early, working through lunch—and the project was completed successfully on schedule. He always put in his share of overtime, though he never let it interfere with his family life. That's rare in the business world. So many executives' lives are consumed by the sometimes cutthroat realities of corporate life. Because of Tim I began to think of who I was outside the job and what I owed to others.

When Tim told me that he would be going into the hospital for gallbladder surgery, I was not too worried about him. After all, this was the twentieth century. Medical science could repair just about anything that might go haywire in the human body, right? Besides, Tim had always seemed in such fine health.

"The doctors tell me it's a pretty routine operation," he assured me over lunch. "But I'll be off my feet for a while, and I won't be coming back to work full time for at least eight weeks. Or so they tell me," he added with a wink. I knew I'd see Tim back in no more than six weeks. I promised I'd pray for him.

While Tim was in the hospital I realized how much I'd come to depend on his attitudes to help straighten out mine. When I was having a problem, I'd usually take it to Tim. In the beginning we just talked about business, but gradually I trusted him enough to talk over more personal matters, such as my marriage or my faith. We both had strong beliefs. Sometimes we'd even pray together. In time I saw that a lot of people around the company felt they could turn to Tim.

And then there were the horses. Our company's headquarters was located outside the city, and Tim's large office looked out on a pasture that usually had some horses grazing in it, beautiful horses. Often Tim and I would pause for a minute or two just to admire those elegant creatures. On hot days they would find a shady place to stand, tails switching. On cooler ones we'd watch them prance and play. On cold days the horses would gather close for warmth. Something about seeing the tranquility of those horses in their pasture gave us a sense of serenity, a glimpse of God at ease in nature.

I was eager for Tim's return and a little surprised that it took him a full two months to recover. I remember being startled to see how his salt-and-pepper hair seemed to have turned mostly salt.

"How are you?" I bubbled that first day, popping my head into his office.

"Fine, Jenny. Great."

"Well, it's great to have you back!"

But some of that old sparkle in Tim's eyes seemed tarnished. *Oh well*, I mused, *surgery is always tough. He'll be okay.*

Gradually, inexplicably, Tim got worse. He lost weight. He barely had the energy to get to work in the morning. Some afternoons I'd peek into his office and Tim's eyes would be closed, his head hung in exhausted sleep. He seemed to age a decade in a matter of months.

Although Tim looked as if the world was beating on him, he didn't talk like it. If I needed advice or help, he was there. I felt a little guilty asking, though. Why should he expend any of his precious energy on my problems? But he did.

A year passed. An important project required Tim and me to fly overseas, the sort of trip that inflicts a nasty case of jet lag on even the hardiest traveler. The strain seemed nearly to kill Tim. He spent every spare minute collapsed on his bed in the hotel. When it came time to give another presentation, he'd pull himself together and perform brilliantly. But I was really getting worried. Then, not long after we got back to Dallas, Tim told me his doctors wanted him to spend two weeks at the Mayo Clinic in Rochester, Minnesota.

"They just don't know what's wrong," he sighed, his voice an exhausted whisper. "I don't have the stamina to have fun with my kids anymore, to help around the house—don't even get out of bed on weekends, don't feel like working, don't feel like anything. I feel like someone just took my life away."

This wasn't the Tim I knew. I could still glimpse a trace of his boyish good looks, but what I saw in his ravaged features was a terrible uncertainty, the kind of fear and vulnerability one sees in a very sick child who doesn't understand why he is suffering. That morning in Tim's office we prayed together, and the next day he left for Mayo.

I'm not sure what the doctors told Tim—I know they put him through a battery of tests—but when he got back he seemed reluctant to talk about it, and he continued to miss a lot of work—more than ever, in fact. I was traveling almost constantly. Between my hectic schedule and Tim's sick days, we barely got a chance to speak. I wanted to tell him about a job offer in New York that I thought I was going to accept. It was a big career move, and I wanted his counsel. But every time I stopped by his office for a chat, all I would see was his neat desk and his empty chair.

Sometimes I would stand at the window gazing at the horses in the meadow. They seemed so content, yet I was so disturbed. I all but wondered out loud to God why innocent humans had to suffer, why Tim was sick. Over and over I'd ask Him to help my friend get better.

I accepted the job in New York, and when the day came for me to leave, I went again to Tim's office, and again he was not there. I taped a note to the back of his chair where he was sure to see it. I was sure I'd see him again.

Not long after I had settled into my new job, I got a call from a friend at my old company in Dallas.

"Jenny," she said, "I have some very bad news. Tim has AIDS. He received contaminated blood during his operation. That's why he never got better."

On the outside I was silent, controlled. I didn't know what to say. But inside I was screaming, *No! No! No!*

"He came in Sunday when no one was here and cleaned out his office. He didn't say good-bye to anyone. People have tried calling him. He just won't talk."

I thanked her and hung up the phone. I wanted to throw it through a wall, but instead I replaced the receiver gingerly in its cradle. *It's just not fair*, I thought.

I decided I shouldn't call Tim. But what could I do for him? I couldn't force him to talk if he didn't want to. So I wrote him a letter instead. I knew that AIDS leaves the victim terribly debilitated. Maybe Tim was too weak to lift up his Bible and read. Along with my letter I included about fifty Bible verses that I'd copied on individual index cards, verses that had to do with hope and faith, suffering and healing, living and dying.

Months went by. I didn't hear from Tim. Not a call, not a note, not a word through a family member. I know now that Tim felt he couldn't face anyone, not even his friends, not even when he was dying. That was one of the most tragic things about AIDS: the stigma, the same irrational feelings that block out compassion, the same fear that in years past made "cancer" a dirty word. Tim must have felt ashamed, deeply ashamed, and afraid of the judgment that even his friends might pass on him.

Early one winter Tim died in Dallas. The funeral was a strictly private family affair, and no mention of the cause of death was cited there or in Tim's obituary, which simply stated that he had died after a "long illness." What the obituary left out was that Tim had died alone and humiliated. I didn't think it was right that my friend, or anyone, should die like that.

I was in my office in New York when I heard the sad news. I stared out my window, thinking, *Oh, Tim, had you turned to us, we would have listened; we would have been there for you just as you were there for us. We wouldn't have blamed you for having the disease; we would have blamed the virus.*

Outside my office window there was no peaceful pasture; there were no gentle, nuzzling horses. Instead there were only tall buildings with glass, and quicksilver elevators, and people like me, ambitious, shooting to the top just as fast as we could because we thought that was what was going to make the vital difference in our lives. I began to cry, not for Tim but for myself.

I felt an emptiness, a sense that my "getting ahead" was only for me, not for God. I'd been demanding to know from God why He had allowed such a horrible thing to happen to my friend. I hadn't received an answer. But sometimes we learn more that way. It wasn't necessary for me to know why God works in the world the way He does. I needed only to know what God wanted of me. Maybe there was nothing I could have done for Tim, but maybe there was something I could do about AIDS.

That day I called a list of organizations dedicated to helping people with AIDS and asked how I could help. I learned there was a lot of work that needed to be done by volunteers like me.

I still work in my field, but only as a part-time consultant. I earn enough to take care of the essentials. I spend the rest of my time taking care of people with AIDS and talking to people who need to know more about AIDS. I give several presentations a week to corporations about AIDS in the workplace and about the nature of the disease in general. I speak to church groups who want to know how they can help. I explain that the disease is not casually or easily transmitted, and that our biggest enemy in the fight against AIDS is fear and ignorance and our greatest need is compassion. For the first time in a long time I feel as if I am doing something Tim's way—not just for myself but for other people and for God.

I still think about Tim. I think a lot about the horses we used to watch in the meadow. I remember how they pranced on nice days, lazed in the shade on hot ones. But mostly I remember how on cold, hard days they came together for warmth. That's the way God intended it for us humans too, I think.

The Way of Love

Love has hands to help others.
It has feet to hasten to the poor and needy.
It has eyes to see misery and want.
It has ears to hear the sighs and sorrows of men.
This is what love looks like.

AUGUSTINE

A Beautiful Friend

BY MARLENE THOMPSON

Helen was different. I'd always known that. Like me, she had Scandinavian roots and the blond looks to prove it. Like mine, her husband was a high achiever, and like mine, her son was an only child. She and I loved people and a good laugh, and mutual friends came to the gatherings in our homes.

I watched my neighbor Helen. I watched her with others, outgoing and charming. I noticed her eagerness to sit and listen whenever someone needed a sympathetic ear. I paid attention to how Helen handled the inevitable crises of an adolescent son, a husband in a high-pressure job, aging parents and illness. She'd shrug and smile and say, "Things will get better. I know."

Helen had hope. And I didn't.

Sometimes on summer weekends Helen and her husband would drive to our beach cottage on the Oregon coast, and my friend and I would slip away from the idle chatter and joking of the group to have a stroll and a serious talk.

My life had always seemed more tumultuous than the ocean's churning, and eventually Helen heard the bitter stories of my unsettled childhood. I confided to Helen some of the fears that plagued my adult life—fears about my being abandoned once again. Fears that somehow I'd end up unwanted and alone.

Helen exuded strength. She looked delicate, but she had a strength that seemed to come from within. When we were together, she calmed my fears and made me feel strong.

Then life for me seemed to splinter apart. My father-in-law lost his life to cancer. My sister developed brain cancer. My marriage of twenty years was crumbling.

Helen knew my anguish. During our phone conversations, her comforting words boosted my crumbling spirits. And she'd gently remind me: "Things will get better, Marlene. I know they will. You'll see."

But I didn't see.

One March day Helen dropped by. She was worried about me. I'd been feeling depressed. We lived on the Willamette River, and some days the thought of walking into the river and sinking to the bottom seemed like the solution. I wanted to die. I think Helen knew that.

"Marlene," she said, "you've been in my thoughts. I can only stay a minute. I just wanted to leave this little gift with you."

Lovely Helen, always thinking of others. Always giving.

I smiled. "You've wrapped this so beautifully, Helen. You're really too good to me.... Oh—" Now that it was unwrapped, I hoped she hadn't noticed my disappointment.

Puzzled, I looked at the gift and tried to sound excited. "A Bible! Just what I need to get myself through these horrible days. How sweet, Helen. Thank you."

I held the small green Bible limply in my hand. Why would I want a Bible? I knew as much about God as I cared to. Look at the forty-one miserable years He'd given me. As soon as Helen left, I tossed the Bible into a drawer.

A year later Helen died.

Things for me became worse. I had a stroke and was hospitalized. Just as I was recovering, my sister died of cancer; her two children, both troubled youngsters, moved into our home. Debts mounted. Then, on New Year's Eve, my husband left.

I was in despair, and on a March day a year later, a day when I longed to die, I began a desperate search for pills. My hands shook as I pulled out one drawer after another.

Where did I put those pills? I asked myself. *Where, where, where?*

And then my groping hand touched something that made me stop short. I brought it out. Helen's Bible. A note dropped from its pages and fell to the floor. I reached down, picked it up, and began to read. The note was addressed to me:

"Marlene, dear, read Psalm Thirty-Four and hang on to its promises. God can't lie! See you soon. Loads of love. Forever your friend, Helen."

Forever my friend. Not even death could restrain Helen's caring spirit. Somehow, here she was again, just when I needed her. Giving me comfort. Telling me I was loved. Pointing me to God.

I turned to Psalm 34. I read it once. "I will bless the LORD at all times..." (verse 1). And I read it again. "I sought the LORD, and He answered me, and delivered me from all my fears" (verse 4). And again. "And none of those who take refuge in Him will be condemned" (verse 22 NASB). And each time I read that beautiful psalm of David I thought of my beautiful friend and her desire for me to find the Lord. It was a beginning, a nudge that sent me in search of Him.

I kept Helen's Bible on the kitchen table as a reminder and a help.

"See you soon," her note had said. And she'd kept that promise—on a day when I needed her most.

Lasting Friendship

True friendships are lasting because true love is eternal. A friendship in which heart speaks to heart is a gift from God, and...all that comes from God participates in God's eternal life.

HENRI J. M. NOUWEN

A Deeper Strength

BY JUNE SCOBEE RODGERS

It's a day that will never be forgotten. January 28, 1986, the day the NASA space shuttle *Challenger*, carrying a seven-member crew, exploded seventy-three seconds after liftoff. An unspeakable tragedy for the nation, for the world. And for me. My husband, Dick Scobee, was the commander at the controls, and for a long time I wasn't sure if I would ever be able to get that day out of my mind.

Nine o'clock, on the morning of the launch. I stood on the rooftop viewing area of the Kennedy Space Center in Merritt Island, Florida, with our son Rich, daughter Kathie, and her son, our first grandchild, Justin. I looked out at the cloudless sky and shivered; it was exceptionally cold for Florida. In the distance I saw the shuttle. Icicles hung from the launchpad. This would be Dick's second spaceflight. He was an experienced Air Force test pilot, had served in Vietnam, and knew how to fly more than forty-five types of aircraft, but I was worried. I was fixated on those icicles.

I thought back to our last conversation, earlier that morning. The four of us were staying at an apartment Dick had rented for us. He was staying in crew quarters. It was still dark when he called. "It's freezing out there," I said. "Is the launch still on?"

"They've given us the go-ahead," he said. "The engineers knocked off icicles they thought might be a problem. They showed us pictures of the rockets blasting off in snow. It's safe, they said."

"Okay," I sighed, not completely convinced. "I love you so much."

"See you in a week," Dick said.

Now here we were, awaiting the big launch. Finally, the countdown began. T-minus ten, nine, eight...liftoff! The floor shook with the raw power of millions of pounds of thrust. We cheered as the shuttle climbed sunward atop a great plume of smoke. Rich put his arms around his sister and me. I turned and smiled at Justin in Kathie's arms. I imagined Dick in his calm, take-charge mode.

All these years later I can still vividly see what came next: the *Challenger* exploded. Flaming debris burst into the perfect sky as the orbiter shattered into a million pieces. *Oh, God! No! Not my husband! Why, God, why?*

My legs wobbled. Rich grabbed my arm to hold me up. In stunned silence, I looked at him, at Kathie. No words came. In one terrible instant our lives had been completely and irrevocably changed. I kept trying to turn the clock back to that last conversation about icicles, as if I could change things. Yet reality kept imposing itself. I was a widow.

A bus took us to crew quarters. There, officials said what we already knew. "The crew's dead. They could not have survived an accident like this."

That night, NASA arranged for us to return to our homes. I dreaded going back to Houston. What was home without Dick? Without my husband, my partner, my best friend and companion for twenty-six blessed, wonderful years?

Somehow I put one foot in front of the other. I made decisions mechanically—memorial services, arrangements for visitors. Inside I was dying, stunned, uncomprehending. I managed to struggle through the weeks following Dick's funeral. Even as the tragedy faded from public view I felt as if I would never really live beyond that moment when the *Challenger* disappeared from the sky.

One afternoon in April, I opened my front door to flashes of lights and questions from reporters about the investigation into the disaster. I froze. "If words could bring back my husband, I would speak volumes," I said, then closed the door and fell to the floor, sobbing. My neighbors Barbara and Fred helped me pack a bag and took me to their home.

Safe in their guest room, I crawled under the bedcovers. My mind was in overdrive, the same thought echoing over and over again: *why?* There was no reason, no acceptable explanation for why my husband was no longer here. I tossed and turned, rubbing my throbbing eyes. How could I go on without Dick? How would I ever feel loved again? *Please, God, let me go to heaven with my husband*, I begged. *But if You won't take me, then give me strength to live.*

I thought back to a time when I felt equally helpless. My dad was an itinerant carpenter. My mother was mentally ill and frequently hospitalized, and though I was a child myself, I was often left in charge of my two younger brothers. I was always anxious. We moved around a lot (fifteen times in ten years) and my grades suffered. I dreamed of escaping our day-to-day struggles, but I saw no way out. One day, when I was nine, a neighbor stopped by with a basket of tangerines and *The Power of Positive Thinking*, which my mother left on our dinette table. I picked it up and started reading. I was mesmerized! Dr. Peale wrote that God was in control of our lives, that He could help us in our times of need. Faith wasn't discussed in our home, but something in me just knew Dr. Peale's words were the truth. From that day on, I prayed. Every night I asked God for strength, for help in rising above my circumstances.

Lying there in bed that April night, I thought about how my life changed dramatically after reading that book. I graduated from high school at sixteen, married Dick, earned a PhD in curriculum and instruction from Texas A&M University, landed a great teaching job, and had two amazing kids and an angel of a grandson. I had been so blessed! *God, You've brought me so far. Can't You help me through this too?* I pleaded. Finally I drifted off.

The next morning, instead of awakening to fear and worry, a deep, indescribable calm fell over me. I heard a voice, not in my ears but in my heart. *It is not your turn. You still have life to live.*

I stepped outside and a ray of sunlight fell across my back. The tense, tight feeling was gone, completely gone. Sounds consoled me—birds singing and children at play, a concord of voices laughing in the distance. A single daffodil bent forward as if to welcome me to spring, to new life. A car drove up—Kathie and Justin. He fell into my arms. "Sweetie!" I shouted, giving him a squeeze. What beauty this life has! How could I ever want to leave it? Leave them? For the first time in a long time, I felt alive and utterly loved.

By summer, the cause of the explosion was found: faulty O-rings had allowed hot gases to leak into the external fuel tank. The *Challenger* families did not want the disaster to be the end of the crew's mission. Soon we unveiled the Challenger Learning Center in Houston—a place where students can climb aboard a child-sized space station and fly a simulated mission. A place I imagined the young Dick Scobees of the world would foster their dreams.

It's still hard to believe what happened that cold, somber January day years ago. But I know that there is life after tragedy and a deeper strength to pull us through.

Our Refuge and Strength

God is our refuge and strength, a very present help in trouble. Therefore we will not fear, though the earth should change and though the mountains slip into the heart of the sea.

PSALM 46:1–2 NASB

A Note from the Editors

Guideposts, a nonprofit organization, touches millions of lives every day through products and services that inspire, encourage, and uplift. Our magazines, books, prayer network, and outreach programs help people connect their faith-filled values to their daily lives. To learn more, visit Guideposts.org.